THE
NISSAN
REPORT

THE NISSAN REPORT

AN INSIDE LOOK AT HOW A
WORLD-CLASS JAPANESE
COMPANY MAKES PRODUCTS THAT
MAKE A DIFFERENCE

Edited by Steve Barnett

HD
9710
.J34
N555
1992

CURRENCY
DOUBLEDAY

NEW YORK   LONDON   TORONTO   SYDNEY   AUCKLAND

A CURRENCY BOOK

PUBLISHED BY DOUBLEDAY
a division of Bantam Doubleday Dell Publishing Group, Inc.
666 Fifth Avenue, New York, New York 10103

CURRENCY and DOUBLEDAY are trademarks of
Doubleday, a division of Bantam Doubleday Dell
Publishing Group, Inc.

Excerpts from the electronic conference hosted by Global
Business Network are included with the permission of the
participants.

Book design by Chris Welch

Library of Congress Cataloging-in-Publication Data

The Nissan report : an inside look at how a world-class
    Japanese company makes products that make a
    difference / edited by Steve Barnett. — 1st ed.
        p.   cm.
    "A Currency book"—T.p. verso.
    1. Nissan Jidōsha Kabushiki Kaisha.   2. Nissan
automobile—Marketing.   I. Barnett, Steve, 1941–
HD9710.J34N555   1992
338.7′6292′0952—dc20   91-31923
                                            CIP

ISBN 0-385-42127-3

Introduction copyright © 1992 by Steve Barnett

Contents

●

The Consumer

· Contents ·

Acknowledgments

●

A conversation via computer is very difficult to organize and to sustain at a high level. I deeply thank those who made it possible, especially Napier Collyns, Joji Doigami, Art Kleiner, JoAnn Magdoff, Don Michael, Danica Remy, and Peter Schwartz. Harriet Rubin and Janet Coleman at Doubleday/Currency saw the possibilities of this innovative format and helped shape its final form.

Foreword

●

A new consumer is rewriting the rules of the marketplace. The greedy "me generation" consumer of the eighties is disappearing; in her place is emerging a more community-focused and responsibility-minded consumer. This new consumer cares not only about a product and what it can do for her (or say about her), she cares about its place in society as well. Increasingly, she wants to know *everything* about the product and its maker—the ingredients and manufacturing techniques employed, the investment and hiring policies of the manufacturer, and the maker's corporate environmental commitment. She makes her purchase decisions only after weighing all of those factors. Indeed, the very word "consumer" seems less and less appropriate for these thoughtful shoppers; "stakeholder," even "partner" might be a better description, as these new buyers have an increasingly powerful impact on the products they purchase.

Coming to terms with these new consumers and their demands is, I believe, the central challenge facing business in the next decade. This book is the result of Nissan's first major step toward that new understanding. It is a conversation, a discussion among remarkable people about what it means to be a "responsible" company. While much of the dialogue turns on automobiles, the lessons that emerge are accessible—and applicable—to organizations of every stripe. It is our hope that this book will be as much help to others as it has been to us; the quality of our lives, not just the quality of our earnings, depends on our learning and adapting to the calls of the new consumer and the new world of which they—and we all—are a part.

The process began for us with Nissan's 1990 strategic plan; as a result of the research that underlay that plan, we came to appreciate the scope of consumers' demands for accountability and responsibility—the extent to which buying was based on values, not simply "value." We realized that this new consumer-as-partner and the new relationship she demands are changing the very definition of the business we are in. To these new consumers, we are not just selling cars (any more than other companies are simply selling soap or hamburgers or long-distance service), we are speaking to their values, their beliefs, their ways of being. We realized that we at Nissan, therefore, are selling *our* beliefs, values, and way of being—as embodied both in our product and in the way we do business. We realized that we needed to be more *responsible*; in the most literal of senses, we needed to develop a sharper "ability to respond" to the emerging new concerns and desires of our customers.

Our first step was to integrate these concerns into our planning process. Planning is essential to the success of any business; but in the auto industry—where we are working, at any point in time, on cars to be introduced in five years—it is critical. We realized that traditional techniques would be of limited help to us; we needed an alternative way to find and understand these emerging concerns, and to understand how to act on them at Nissan. Most fundamentally, our problem was the sheer complexity of the issues at hand. It was a relatively simple thing to realize that the new consumer "cares"; but the ways in which she cares—and the responses appropriate to a company like Nissan—were anything but clear.

My group at Nissan North America, the Strategic Planning Group, decided that we had no choice but to embrace that complexity. We did not assemble the expected cadre of MBA's or product designers; we wanted to avoid reductive, business-as-usual responses. Instead, we turned to an unusual consulting firm, the Global Business Network, a scenario planning group that had worked with us on the 1990 plan. With GBN we assembled a group of ecologists, business planners, physicists, community leaders, even an astronaut, to talk about what it means to be a responsible company. Because our participants were spread around the world, we linked them electronically, via computer and modem; for *six* weeks, participants logged in at any time of the day or night to join the conversation.

The result of that teleconference is this book. The contents are grouped into themes for more coherent reading; otherwise, they are unchanged. What is important is the flow of the conversation, for this is a book with no safe nor simple conclusions.

Still, within Nissan, the ideas unleashed in our teleconference have begun to change the way we do business. At the broadest level, we have initiated many fundamental product changes; we have begun a program to make our manufacturing process more environmentally sound; and we have begun a program to communicate much more quickly and openly with our consumers. More specific action resulted as well, for example:

- We realized that we did not fully appreciate the way that our customers actually understand and use our cars, so we initiated a project using tape recordings of owners made while they are driving. That real-time understanding of what matters to drivers has led us to a number of major design changes.
- We began to understand that our customers don't fit neatly into tightly defined "boxes," so we revised our customer-segmentation model to allow for "fuzzy clustering"—to allow a single customer to fit into a number of different segments, depending on which aspect of consumption is being stressed.
- We concluded that our sense of an appropriate product range was too narrow, so we have begun serious investigation of a number of new types of electric vehicles, and have developed a uniquely fast rechargeable battery.

We undertook this project for Nissan's benefit. But precisely because it was of such tremendous use to us, we have agreed to publish it. We believe that the conversation in this book can be as powerful a stimulant for other companies as it has been for ours. And we believe that it is our responsibility to share it. Anyone who buys, manufactures, or sells will find here a compelling portrait of the new forces at play in the business environment. The new consumer wants products and services that speak to her conscience and her aesthetics as well as to her pocketbook. Companies that want successfully to serve this new consumer must reexamine *all* of their assumptions about doing business. This book begins that process by investigating, in turn, the evolving consumer, product, corporation, and business environment.

It will take a new kind of company to meet the demands of this evolution in the nineties and beyond. We hope that this book will start that change in other organizations, as it has within Nissan.

Steve Barnett
New York City

Introduction

●

In the spirit of the conversation that is this book, and of the conversations within other companies that we hope it will start, we begin with an interview in which I talk with Lawrence Wilkinson of GBN. We met in San Francisco to discuss the broad implications of my work at Nissan. (Since that time, having built the planning function at Nissan, I left to resume my practice as an independent consultant in strategic planning and consumer values.)

LW: What's a nice young cultural anthropologist like you doing at a car company?

STEVE BARNETT (SB): I'm not preoccupied with cars as cars. That makes me strange in the company. Of course, everybody around me talks cars, they fix cars, they claim to derive pleasure from driving them. I say "claim" because I don't know if that's true. But, for me, all the car is is a central symbol in our culture. And so, if I am going to feel I'm doing something other than the crass earning of money, something that is somehow relevant to the lives we live, then working, doing strategic planning, in a company that is making a central product seems interesting. So that's why I'm in a car company. And I also think that, in addition to being symbolically central, cars are also environmentally, behaviorally, and organizationally central. Working in a car company in Los Angeles, looking out the window at the smog . . . you almost feel like some kind of criminal. So having helped move Nissan in the direction of responsibility is personally satisfying.

LW: Say a bit about what you've been able to initiate at Nissan. What does being the director of Strategic Planning for Nissan North America consist of?

SB: I wear two hats; one is a research hat. My group does all the research that is oriented toward understanding the consumer and where the consumer is going. One of the things I do is try to innovate in research. Most business research is terrible. It's mostly bad surveys, bad questions, no thinking about hypotheses, no thinking about deeper structure—just the mindless accumulation of numbers. I have the luxury of creating many strange research projects. For example, we're working right now on trying to understand if people get into a "flow state" in automobiles; we're working with Professor Cziskzentmihalyi at the University of Chicago. We also try to look at the car as a system of symbols—for many people, the most important part of the car is the steering wheel, oddly enough. That's what they touch, that's what they manipulate to feel in control—the thickness, the feel of it, conveys to them the whole symbology of the automobile. In fact one of the things I've done at Nissan is to create a diagram of the car for engineers from a consumer's standpoint, in which the steering wheel is proportionally big and the engine is small.

The second thing I do is planning. Nissan did not have

xviii

any organized strategic planning in the U.S. before my group was established. So I'm not only doing strategic planning in a business sense, but I'm developing the idea of strategic planning for Nissan. Which means much dialogue with various executives about what it means to plan—why it's important, why it's anything other than a pain in the ass . . . I think good strategic planning is by definition a pain in the ass. So I have this fundamental discussion all the time about what the company is about.

LW: The experts on biology, physics, aesthetics you've assembled in The Nissan Report advise you on cars, yet your interest is in new products and their value—in a way that charts the conditions of the new marketplace.

SB: I started out not especially knowledgeable about cars (although now I am unfortunately knowledgeable about them, so much so that friends tell me, "Enough car talk!"). I've been able to exclude what I call the bias in strategic planning—that is, the bias that says, "We know our business, we've been in this business for a long time, and so I can look at this prototype and tell you if the design works, just by looking at it; just because I'm an experienced guy, I can look at this and tell you whether in 1996 this will sell or not."

It is a question of shifting emphasis—from how you can embellish the products you know and love to how you can get inside the consumer's head and figure out what she really wants—even if it means completely redefining your business. What I say when people ask me is, "I have no idea what detailed, specific design we'll sell in 1996. Let's look at some other things around the car, let's not just be car guys." Car guys are right half the time and wrong half the time— the same guys who said Edsel said Mustang. So I've been able to exclude what I call the bias of the industry, which is, I think, often limiting.

LW: What you're doing—this combination of research and planning—you're doing in Los Angeles. And as so much of your research is focused on the symbolic content of the experience of automobiles (when people buy cars, they buy more than machinery, they buy a tangible expression of their own values), I'm wondering what it is like to be doing that work in the "symbol capital of the world." As you raise your eyes and look at that context, what do you see evolving in the "symbolic economy"?

SB: I am torn between two ways of looking at symbols. One follows the thinking of Jean Baudrillard, that surface is everything; to look beneath the surface at this point is to make an analytic error, because people are only at the surface and that's what they are manipulating. The second—and my intellectual training is in this kind of symbolic thinking—is very deeply structural. That is, always to look for the unstated: anything that means something to somebody leaves something unsaid, and the unsaid part will give you Sherlock Holmesean clues to what's going on. Which, in a sense, is the basis of anthropology: you go someplace else because you can think through what is unsaid in another culture by bouncing it off your own experience. In Los Angeles, I must confess, I expected that the symbol as surface would be accentuated, but it's been the deep structural part. I see a lot of movement toward fractionation as having very deep roots. In fact, I was listening yesterday to PBS and a commentator was talking about the fact that we don't see whole people any more in ads, we see elbows, buttocks, ears; the person is beginning to break apart, and different meanings are associated with different parts of the person. That symbolic breaking apart, where ever more meanings are packed into ever smaller units, is what I see in Los Angeles. For example, it used to be that a sportscar, with all its symbolic connotations of luxury, adventure, and driving skill, was a complex machine that fulfilled specific performance and design criteria. Now, the idea of sportscar can be conveyed solely by a thick, leather, padded steering wheel. Put this kind of steering wheel in a Volkswagen Rabbit, and the driver will feel like he is in the Grand Prix. I don't simply see this as surface, I see it as a longer-term shift in our society. I happen to believe there are Kondra-tieff-like long cultural curves, even though there are proba-bly not Kondratieff-like long economic cycles. . . . So I take him as a metaphor. I think that we're coming to the end of a long cycle that placed the emphasis on the person as the minimal unit of being, or the minimal symbol, à la enlightenment thought. We're seeing the breaking apart of that. That's taken place over many years.

LW: Where do you see these dynamics leading? Can you elaborate on other ways in which the wave is crashing? And what is the impact on the marketplace?

SB: Well, the trendy phrase is awful, but it's "demassifica-tion," which leads to the ultimate in customized products. Instead of taking whatever rolls off the assembly line, cus-tomers will demand a say in every aspect of design and manufacturing. That has both tremendous potential and also a grotesque aspect. The grotesque aspect is the *Fahren-heit 451* component, where Julie Christie gets to the end of the banal TV soap opera and gets to choose her "own, personal, participatory" conclusion. We're already at the point of choosing endings. There are some films now in which, as they're prescreened to consumers, endings get chosen based on audience votes. This idea of "roll your own" has a grotesque aspect. We are not all designers; we are not all writers of fiction. If we create everything ourselves—and technology is clearly moving to make that possible—we are likely to create some of the ugliest, most banal crap the world has ever seen.

Archaeologists will marvel in the future at these relics. So there is an aspect of demassification that to me is a little daunting—it's almost antieducation. That is, one need not learn, suffer, struggle to produce something, one must merely flick a technological switch and it is produced. I design my own sweater on a computer screen, the screen then translates my design into knitting instructions. Two weeks later I get the sweater. All well and good, except I don't know how to design a sweater.

Participants

●

PETER WARSHALL is a maniacal naturalist with specialties in water resources, community balances of conservation and development, and wildlife. He has worked from Ethiopia to Senegal (across the Sahel), Botswana, Chile, Mexico, and throughout North America. He writes on natural resource management, environmental impacts, and Mount Graham red squirrels. He works as a private consultant (Tohono O'odham Nation, UNEP, UNDP, U.S. AID, Biosphere2, Volvo, Nissan, SAS, Trygg Hansa, etc.) and is a research associate with the Office of Arid Lands Studies, University of Arizona. He acts as researcher for a sewage treatment plant that utilizes water hyacinths to clean influent, and is project director of the wastewater management study for the City of Malibu, California. He writes for *Whole Earth Review, Orion, Shelter,* and other magazines. Mr. Warshall has a PhD in biological anthropology from studying rhesus monkey behavior, and a degree in cultural anthropology from the École Pratique des Hautes Études (Paris).

In April 1991, **KEES VAN DER HEIJDEN** was appointed professor of strategic management at the Graduate Business School of Strathclyde University, Glasgow. Prior to his teaching position, he was in charge of Shell's scenario planning as head of the Business Environment Division of Group Planning, Royal Dutch/Shell, London. In this capacity he was responsible for monitoring and analysing the business environment and communicating with top management on strategic implications. He has worked in Group Planning in London since 1980, previously as head of Internal Strategy Consultancy. Van der Heijden is an engineering graduate of the University of Delft, the Netherlands.

RUSSELL L. (RUSTY) SCHWEICKART is the president of NRS Communications, Inc., an international computer and communications firm specializing in international communications links. He is best known as the lunar module pilot for Apollo 9, March 3–13, 1969, logging 241 hours in space. He also served as backup commander for the first Skylab mission, which flew in the spring of 1973. Schweickart was awarded the NASA Distinguished Service Medal (1969) and the Federation Aeronautique Internationale De La Vaulx Medal (1970) for his Apollo 9 flight. He also received the National Academy of Television Arts and Sciences Special Trustees Award (Emmy) in 1969 for transmitting the first live IV pictures from space. In 1973 Schweickart was awarded the NASA Exceptional Service Medal for his leadership role in the Skylab rescue efforts. Schweickart is the founder and past president of the Association of Space Explorers (ASE), the international professional society of astronauts and cosmonauts. He is a fellow of the American Astronautical Society and the International Academy of Astronautics, and an associate fellow of the American Institute of Aeronautics and Astronautics. He received his

x
x
i
v

bachelor of science degree in 1956 and his master of science degree in 1963, both from the Massachusetts Institute of Technology.

The president and cofounder of Global Business Network, PETER SCHWARTZ has focused on two major areas of research —energy resources and the environment. He has anticipated major technical change in these fields and has developed effective business strategies. Prior to GBN, Schwartz was the head of Business Environment for the Royal Dutch/Shell Group of companies in London. From 1982 to 1986, he led a team of thirty-five that developed a comprehensive analysis of the global business environment and worked with the senior management to apply scenario planning to the company's strategic concerns. From 1980 to 1981, Schwartz was the director of the Strategic Environment Center at Stanford Research Institute (now SRI International).

Peter Schwartz has coauthored *Seven Tomorrows* with James Ogilvy and Paul Hawken (1982), *Energy Futures, Human Values and Lifestyles* (1982), and *The Art of the Long View* (Doubleday/Currency, May, 1991). He has a BS in Aeronautical Engineering and Astronautics from Rensselaer Polytechnic Institute.

DR. JOHN ROZSA is head of Scenario Planning for the California Energy Commission. Previously, Dr. Rozsa directed the Commission's Fuels Planning Program, which prepares the *Fuels Report*, California's long-range fuels policy strategy document. Prior to joining the Commission, Dr. Rozsa was a consultant to the federal government on energy information and transportation systems while research manager at Transportation and Energy Research Associates in Arlington, Virginia. Earlier, he was a professor of management and organizational behavior at the University of Maryland's University College. Raised in Los Angeles, Dr. Rozsa received his PhD from the University of Texas at Austin in social psychology. He also holds a bachelor of arts degree in mathematics from the University of California, Los Angeles. Dr. Rozsa lives with his family in Sacramento where he is active in Odyssey of the Mind, an international creative problem-solving competition for young people. He is currently coauthoring a book on strategic planning in government entitled *Entrepreneurial Government: Strategic Planning in the Public Sector.*

DANICA REMY organized this conference for Nissan. In her position at GBN, Danica is responsible for organizing meetings, electronic conversations, publications, and computer operations. She has taught the use of computers for fifteen years. Danica coordinated a private series of conferences on "Learning in Complex Systems," sponsored by planners at Royal Dutch/Shell, AT&T, and Volvo. Her other positions include associate producer of several independent feature films, coordinator of Lucasfilms' post-release film quality control program, film festival manager, data collector for social welfare studies, and a hotel operations manager.

NANCY RAMSEY is president of Morning Star Imports. Ramsey is the former legislative director to Senator John Kerry. Before joining the senator's staff Ramsey served as president of Ramsey Associates, a Washington-based consulting firm specializing in arms control, international affairs, and national security. Ramsey cofounded and directed the Committee for National Security. She also served as director of Americans for SALT, legislative director for the Women's International League for Peace and Freedom, assistant to the director of the National Welfare Rights Organization, staff assistant to the Governor of Massachusetts, and with the Commonwealth Service Corps. Ramsey has served on a number of boards of directors including the Women's Campaign Fund, the Na-

xxvi

tional Peace Academy Campaign, and Peace Links International. She currently serves on the board of the Fund for Constitutional Government. She is a coauthor of *Nuclear Weapons Decision Making* (Macmillan, London, England), has been a contributor to *In the Public Interest,* and is a member of the Club of Rome. In 1984 she was a Distinguished Resource Fellow at the Center for Conflict Resolution at George Mason University. Ramsey is a graduate of Colby College and received a master's degree in social work from the University of Chicago.

ELSA PORTER is a consultant, teacher, and writer. She is vice president of the Maccoby Group, Washington, D.C., and a former U.S. Assistant Secretary of Commerce. Porter was coauthor of *What Works: The New Business Logic* and *Responsibility Systems*, both video-based learning programs. She pioneered the development of innovative administrative practices that improve both productivity and the quality of work life. A graduate of Harvard's Kennedy School of Government, she is a fellow of the National Academy of Public Administration and is currently chairing a study on how to preserve for history the federal government's growing electronic databases.

JAMES PELKEY is a private investor. Prior experience includes: general partner of Montgomery Securities responsible for venture capital investing; President of Sorcim, a personal computer software company; manufacturer of voice processing equipment Digital Sound Corporation; and a consulting company focusing on computer software, communications, and computer graphics. Current boards are: Digital Sound Corporation, MCAE Technologies, Global Business Network, Peregrine Partners, and the Santa Fe Institute.

IAN I. MITROFF is the Harold Quinton Distinguished Professor of Business Policy and the director of the USC Center for Crisis Management at the Graduate School of Business, University of Southern California, Los Angeles. He has published eleven books and over two hundred papers dealing with current events, strategic planning, crisis management, national defense, and organizational psychiatry. He is also a GBN Network Member.

DON MICHAEL is emeritus professor of planning as public policy and psychology, University of Michigan. In the 1970s he wrote *On Learning to Plan—And Planning to Learn*, a groundbreaking study of organizational learning. Learning, says Michael, has become an ethical imperative because traditional answers are no longer effective in today's turbulent world. He's been writing and talking this up as educator, administrator, and consultant ever since.

PAMELA McCORDUCK is the author and coauthor of seven books, many of them focused on aspects of artificial intelligence. Among them are *Machines Who Think, The Fifth Generation,* and *Aaron's Code.* Her work has been translated into most major European and Asian languages. She is currently working on a personal memoir.

ART KLEINER writes a column on corporate environmentalism for *Garbage* magazine, and is a frequent contributor to *Harvard Business Review, New York Times Magazine,* and the *San Francisco Bay Guardian.* Formerly an editor of *Whole Earth Review,* he now lives in Oxford, Ohio, where he is writing *The Age of Heretics,* (to be published by Doubleday), a history of efforts to change large corporations for the better during the past twenty years.

KEVIN KELLY spent eight years during the 1970s riding local buses in Asia. He is currently on sabbatical from editorship of *Whole Earth Review,* writing a book on how machines are becoming biological, and how complex systems evolve.

JACK HUBER was born in Louisville, Kentucky, and earned BEE, ME, and MBA degrees at the University of Louisville. He is currently a trustee of the Marketing Science Institute, and a member of the advisory board of the Marketing Research Master's Degree Program at the University of Georgia. His work experience includes marketing, new service development, marketing research, regulatory affairs, engineering, and planning with AT&T and BellSouth. He is currently Director of Market Intelligence and Analysis for BellSouth Services.

CHUCK HOUSE, Senior Vice President of Product Management and Development at Informix Software, has been deeply involved with questions of technology and their impact on society for many years. He developed and taught a course at Stanford on "Information Systems and Their Impact on Society," which was prototyped on the National Technological University satellite network for a PBS proposal. He founded and is president of InnovaScapes, a consulting firm concerned with issues of creativity, innovation, and societal infrastructures. House was associated with Hewlett-Packard for many years, in a variety of technical and management roles, including five years as corporate engineering director. He is also a GBN Network Member.

BARBARA HEINZEN is a freelance analyst and a research associate at the School of Oriental and African Studies in London. In the past five years she has written a series of reports on the long-term futures of China, Japan, Latin America, and Europe for member companies of Royal/Dutch Shell. She is currently working on a book about how both advanced and developing countries grow.

PETER H. GLEICK is the director of the Global Environment Program of the Pacific Institute for Studies in Development, Environment, and Security in Berkeley, California. Dr.

xxix

Gleick received his BS from Yale University in engineering and applied science, and his MS and PhD from the Energy and Resources Group of the University of California, Berkeley. He received a MacArthur Foundation Research and Writing Fellowship in 1988 to look at the implications of climatic changes for international water resources and international security. From 1980 to 1982, he served as Deputy Assistant for Energy and Environment to the Governor of California. Dr. Gleick has published extensively on global environmental issues, including the greenhouse effect, climate change, and water resources, and the links between global environmental problems and international politics.

GRAHAM GALER works in Group Planning, Shell International Petroleum Company Limited, London, UK. His division assists Royal Dutch/Shell Group management teams and their planners, sometimes with the support of external consultants, in the development of strategy and of strategic planning processes. Galer has been closely associated with the use of scenario planning methods, and has worked on consultancy projects in a number of Shell's international businesses and national operating companies, especially in Europe, South America, and the Far East. He holds a degree in mathematics and economics from Cambridge University.

GERARD FAIRTLOUGH graduated from Cambridge University in 1953 and joined the Royal Dutch/Shell Group of companies, where he worked for twenty-five years. His final position was as managing director of Shell Chemicals UK Limited. In 1978 he joined the newly formed National Enterprise Board as a divisional director. In 1980, he helped create the biotechnology company Celltech Limited, serving as its chief executive until his retirement in 1990. In 1991 Mr. Fairtlough was appointed member of the Council for National

Academic Awards. He was awarded the CBE in 1989 and has honorary DSc degrees from City University and the Council for National Academic Awards.

PETER COYOTE is a film and TV actor and former chair of the California Arts Council. He is also a GBN Network Member.

NAPIER COLLYNS joined Global Business Network in 1988. Previously he was the Director of Public Affairs for the Atlantic Refining and Marketing Corporation. From 1979 to 1986, he served as the Vice President of Public Affairs and Corporate Planning for Scallop Corporation, a Royal Dutch/Shell company. Mr. Collyns is a graduate of Cambridge University with a major in history, specializing in economic history. He also has a master's degree from Brown University in American civilization, with a special interest in the history of science.

DOUG CARMICHAEL is a physicist turned psychoanalyst, anthropologist, and consultant, and a partner in Metasystems Design Group in Arlington, Virginia, emphasizing electronic conferencing. Mixing the human and the technical in an ever wider web of ambivalences, he keeps his humor and hope that in the balance the human will develop so as to maintain parity. Carmichael has a PhD in developmental psychology from the University of California, Berkeley.

STEWART BRAND is best known for founding, editing, and publishing the *Whole Earth Catalog* (1968–85; National Book Award, 1972). He is cofounder of two companies, the WELL, a computer teleconference system, and Global Business Network, an international think tank and consulting group; and one magazine, the *Whole Earth Review*. Brand has written extensively and been involved with the development of computers and the media arts. His books include *Two Cybernetic Frontiers* (Random House, 1974) and *The Media Lab: Inventing the Future at*

MIT (Viking, 1987). He is on the board of trustees of the Santa Fe Institute, which studies chaos theory and complex adaptive systems, has a degree in biology from Stanford, 1960, and two years experience as a U.S. Infantry officer.

MARY CATHERINE BATESON is a cultural anthropologist who is currently working on a book on learning throughout the life cycle, and is Clarence Robinson Professor in Anthropology and English at George Mason University in Virginia. Bateson began her career studying Middle Eastern linguistics and branched into the more general study of patterns of communication and value systems. Her best known books are *Composing a Life,* a study of the way in which discontinuities are bridged and multiple commitments harmonized by some contemporary American women, and *With a Daughter's Eye: A Memoir of Margaret Mead and Gregory Bateson.* Her interest in ecological issues goes back to a 1972 publication, *Our Own Metaphor,* which was recently reissued by the Smithsonian Institute.

For the past thirteen years, STEVE BARNETT has worked as a strategic planner, linking consumer trends and emerging technology. As the head of his own consulting company, he contributed to the consumer strategies of major U.S. and global corporations. Most recently he served as director of product and market strategy for Nissan North America. Before his business career, he taught social science at Princeton, Brown, and MIT. He has a PhD in anthropology, and has published extensively on consumer and social trends.

THE

CONSUMER

1

Getting to the Heart of a Marketing Problem

●

PAMELA McCORDUCK: I'm having some trouble with the notion of [individual] "responsibility." It once seemed so clear: do your duty, which, of course, was well defined. Now responsibility seems contingent: a responsible act yesterday is irresponsible today. Perhaps the most responsible decision I ever made was to decline to have children. But how many would choose that? And I didn't make that choice very high-mindedly.

STEVE BARNETT: "Responsibility" can then become a metaphor for Christian-like guilt: no matter what you do, it's not enough. Can we then imagine being guilt-free consumers? Is there a guilt-free driving experience, or is it fundamentally tainted?

DON MICHAEL: Pamela, I wonder whether in many cases the intersection of hyperinformation with a vast range of options (products, symbols, life ways) affects the making of responsible choices, as follows:

For folks aware of the alternatives and contingencies,

usually it is just too damn complicated (that is, time-consuming and conflict-full) to brood over what is a responsible choice. So we throw up our hands and either say, "Whatever!" or we focus in on a limited set of criteria (ideology, belief, peer behavior, etc.) and go for it, knowing—guiltily, Steve?—that there is more to things. Occasionally, as in your example, the act of deciding is worth all one can put into it. But how many decisions in a world like this are persons prepared to see as so life-encompassing? Not many, I think.

Then there are the folks who live in a less self-conscious world of responsibility-based choices in which life is simpler—and advertising helps to make it so. The future is not much of a criterion for present choices. The same set of simplifying references as above operates here, but without a sense of despairing retreat: these just are the way one chooses.

My sense is that most folks are not likely to be genuinely caught up in serious self-questioning about whether they're being responsible in a complex situation which they probably don't even perceive as complex.

PAMELA McCORDUCK: "Hyper-info against a vast range of options = indifference." That's for sure. If you're asking for a theological struggle every time I pick up a package of toilet tissue in the grocery, forget it. Like any sensible person, I reserve that kind of moral wrestling for life decisions. I fear most consumers in the world fall into the second category. Life is simpler that way.

So, can an automobile manufacturer, in its own long-term self-interest of self-sustainability, make some decisions for me, or at least narrow the search space? That is, if a manufacturer informed me that, as a corporate entity, it had

4

commissioned studies/run simulations/kept an advisory board in progress on such topics, and, in its opinion, had designed a responsible car, I'd listen. Given our pervasive skepticism, I'd probably want to know that backup material was available if I wished it (reports, etc.) but I'd consider a claim like that closely.

I am not impressed that such a manufacturer meets government standards. Who doesn't? Many American auto manufacturers have shamed us all with their whining and niggling about government standards—put it off for just another year, please—but even they eventually capitulate.

STEWART BRAND: And if there's an advisory board, one wants some proof that it is listened to, since the customary way for government to avoid any action whatsoever on an issue is to appoint a blue-ribbon commission to study the matter.

DON MICHAEL: It's not only who would believe all those studies (not only the ones from auto companies), but how much of the population can evaluate what they are told and how much gives a damn?

PAMELA McCORDUCK: "Advisory board as a way of evading real action." Yes, afraid that's true. I was assuming action had been taken by our mythical Responsible Auto Company, and they were touting their advisory board as the reason why.

PETER SCHWARTZ: Responsibility implies some capacity to understand causal connections between what we do and the outcomes of our behavior—both intended and unintended. I am impressed with how many people, for example, see cars and gasoline, rather than driving, as the source of pollution. It is not their behavior that is seen as the cause of pollution.

As a civilization, I think we have focused on the morality

5

of intentions rather than on the morality of outcomes. Hence, people avoid using paper diapers because it makes them feel good, not because they understand the real environmental trade-offs between paper and cloth. My question is how much of this is denial and how much is lack of information?

STEWART BRAND: Peter, are you perhaps suggesting it is easier to be "responsible" about clear issues? About former issues on which there is now consensus?

DON MICHAEL: Denial, yes. It's a powerful way to fend off information!

2

Who Really Cares About Environmentalism?

●

DON MICHAEL: How well can we depend on a significant population to continue to place high value on environmental concerns and to act on these values responsibly? More specifically, will environmental questions continue to preoccupy enough people to interest car makers in bringing a "responsible" car to market?

I don't get a clear sense of what we believe to be the norms of responsibility which different kinds of people *may* bring to their decision to buy this car or that one, over the next fifteen or twenty years. We have implied some of what might be operating, but mostly I sense that we have been examining our own criteria for "responsibility" or arguing about what should be the criteria.

But what do we think they will be for other segments of the car-purchasing population in the U.S. and Europe, for example?

In our discussion, we have not mentioned the worldwide studies of levels of moral development by Lawrence Kohlberg. He has developed a six-part scale running from: "If you can get away with it, it's okay," to a sophisticated bringing of conscience to bear on moral challenges. (I'm crudely paraphrasing here.) Substantial numbers of people subscribe to one or another level. (The arguments and research of his former student, Carol Gilligan, showing that women make moral choices by different criteria than does Kohlberg's all-male sample, simply add more bases for moral choices.)

Perhaps there is no underlying cultural consensus, especially in heterogeneous societies like the U.S.

STEWART BRAND: Don, I continue to be startled at how rapidly the current public frenzy for environmental issues broke upon us (and I don't really trust it yet, either: often, the storm that comes fast goes fast). To me, it's a warning of how rapidly the mass market can shift its values —tough for a manufacturer with a how-many-year lead time?

DOUG CARMICHAEL: Chernobyl and recent earthquakes indicate that the public will learn to accept major catastrophes as a matter of life. Will the public get cynical and accept a dirty world and get on with it?

STEWART BRAND: Don't forget the end of the Cold War and of nuclear angst.

Two effects: one, everybody still has a "habit of dread"; two, they look at the next item down the list, global warming, which translates into general environmental angst.

Also going on, the pernicious desire for a risk-free world. And "environment" brings along a pretty "mature" set of concerns—much of the research has been done, the wicked named, the curricula written and okayed . . . E-Z, Off-the-Shelf issues. The convenience of this last item is also handy for corporations who want to respond quickly.

CATHERINE BATESON: Those of us who have been thinking about the environment for thirty years or so need to watch our responses to the new wave of environmentalism with some care.

On the one hand, there is a tendency to be snobbish about new converts which we really can't afford. I wish a popular and effective environmentalism really were an off-the-shelf matter. Most political achievements fall short of the original ideal, but the tacky reality is what shapes the future. And then there are a lot of real anxieties we need to have about the emerging popularization: Will it burn out? Will it lead to a kind of tokenism? Will it lead to palliatives that are regarded as achievements? Will it lead to polarization, particularly on rich-poor lines?

ART KLEINER: Stewart's comment just made me suspect that, if people believe that nuclear war is indeed less of a threat, they're more inclined to want to plan for the future. That includes corporate executives.

CATHERINE BATESON: Stewart has suggested that the current environmental surge is angst replacement. I want to suggest an alternative possibility. Perhaps globalism was genuinely impossible for many people as long as half the planet was conceived as enemy territory. You cannot worry about the warming of half the globe—but how to worry about the warming of the whole globe when:

a) this will help your enemies, and

b) your self-restraint will involve a cost which you feel sure your wicked enemies will not incur?

Now, probably no one in this group thinks that way, but if others think so, then it's very important. Another impor-

9

tant factor: the discovery that Eastern-bloc nations have a worse environmental record than we do. But that's parenthetical to the more general point that the new environmentalism may represent a new globalism for folk who are just tuning in to the concept of "one world."

3

Social Values and the Marketplace

●

DON MICHAEL: If being "responsible" requires taking the future seriously, how is a politically and economically relevant population to be moved into that mind/action condition? (I mean a population large enough to assure the laws and possess the pocketbooks to make it worthwhile for an auto producer to produce a responsible car.)

My own work (with the Committee on Disaster Studies of the National Research Council) corroborates Doug's speculation about the general response to disasters: "The public will learn to accept major catastrophes as a matter of life. Will the public get cynical and ignore a dirty world and get on with it?"

People don't so much get cynical as they deny the threat of reoccurrence, explain away the past, and just plain adapt. Remember, we are the adaptable creature par excellence: "We have air conditioners; biotech will take care of the rest . . . ; anyhow, the scientists don't agree [on environmental destruction], and even if it's [coming], it's a long way off."

CATHERINE BATESON: Increasingly, people are being asked not to go and do what needs to be done and do it well, but to meet narrowly defined criteria and be blind to everything else. What is the conceptual change that would allow me to regard the survival of a species of squirrel or owl as relevant to my purposes? To Nissan's purposes?

JACK HUBER: Looking at responsible [attitudes], there seem to be two at least—passive, "Sorry, they are to blame"; and active, "What can/should we do?"

What should/can Nissan do? There seem to be other aspects of "responsibility" besides environmentalism. For example:

- technical design for safety; we still slaughter 50,000 people per year.
- integrity/quality: for maintenance, dependability, upkeep, accessibility, use for and by the disabled.
- recyclability: the ability to change, modify, reuse, without discarding (junking).
- styling for longevity, not planned obsolescence.
- comfort/perks, to enjoy.

Perhaps these last two are not important to us personally —someone already suggested that this group is not average. Did they say we are elite? But these elements are important to Joe and Sue Six-Pack, as well as to Sonja and Eric Perrier. And, after all, these folks do buy all of this stuff, don't they?

DON MICHAEL: As for better safety design, half those car

deaths are drinking-related. Responsibility? Most car deaths happen to folks under twenty-five, if I remember rightly. Responsibility? Go for it!

JACK HUBER: Don, should we or Nissan or "X" depend on the whims of the average Joe or Sue, or the drunk, or the reckless? It doesn't strike me that they are going to be necessarily interested in either responsibility or environmentalism. But supposing a responsible company came up with a strategy which combined the benefits of responsibility, the attractiveness of bells and whistles and buttons and bows, and the effectiveness of environmentalism?

The "alky" [alcoholic] might be handled with an onboard voice test against a print, or the push-button things they [car companies] are testing.

Seems to me, though, that people are less likely to resent being made to be responsible when they want to be independent, if the responsibility is concealed. Hey, when's the last time you guys/gals went cruising, with the idea of being "responsible"?

DON MICHAEL: We readily admit that most corporations do not act responsibly in a systemic way. What is the way most individuals who buy cars perceive their responsibility? Surely they are as nonsystemic as the corporations?

Barbara has suggested an approach to this: think about someone you know well and whose life ways suggest a different sense of what it is to be responsible. What might they tell you/us about how other car buyers may make their choices over the next ten or twenty years?

PAMELA McCORDUCK: I know a surprising number of people who buy cars for reasons I wouldn't. My mother keeps buying Buicks because she's always bought Buicks, and anyway she likes/feels sorry for the guy who sells them to her. For many people in the U.S., there is serious dealer loyalty, regardless of the merits of the car.

For a while, my stepdaughter wouldn't consider buying a foreign car—it would be "taking jobs away from Americans." Subsequently, she has needed more reliability than she could hope for in an American car, and now drives a Honda.

My siblings take the attitude that practical cars are for practical things; toys are for playtime. One immediate filter for me in buying a car is how close geographically a dealer is. I value my time, and the greatest car in any and all dimensions would not impel me to buy it if I had to go to a lot of trouble to get it serviced. Which refers back to my concentric-circle model of car buyers' concerns, i.e., what is important to the buyer personally—whether safety, good gas mileage, or stylishness matters most, followed by other things that matter less.

GRAHAM GALER: A couple of comments about consumers:

1. In the U.K. a very substantial percentage of the cars on the road are provided by organizations for their employees. This is also the case in Australia, I believe. The organizations concerned are not only commercial companies but also governmental groups, including local authorities and some school boards. Due to (past) high levels of marginal-income taxation in the U.K., commercial organizations began to resort to providing cars as a nonsalary element of the compensation package, and the practice spread. Although tax rates are now lower, a system has grown up which is resistant to change due to the vested interests of the various players within it.

Most people with company cars acquire the largest car which their status permits, regardless of need. They often drive fast and aggressively. Since they do not pay for maintenance, they do not worry too much about treating their car with care. Company-car drivers constitute a goodly proportion of the single drivers in large cars who may be seen clogging up London's roads during the rush hours.

Are these people (I am one of them) irresponsible consumers? Are they just taking rational decisions on the basis of the information available to them within the system in which they find themselves?

2. In Germany there is no speed limit on the autobahns. High-performance cars may often be seen doing 120 mph-plus. (You see them in the U.K. and France, too, but there they are breaking the law!) Some of these drivers are clearly irresponsible, because they scare the daylights out of more sedate drivers and hence jeopardize safety. But in many cases they are driving safely and well within the safety margins of their superbly engineered vehicles (which are sometimes equipped with catalytic converters!). Are they responsible consumers, provided they buy (or their companies buy) legally authorized cars and drive them within the highway regulations? Or do they have some higher responsibility toward society which ought to cause them to drive more slowly?

And are the companies which make these high-performance cars (which includes some respected Japanese companies) acting responsibly?

KEES VAN DER HEIJDEN: "Company cars." This is very popular in the U.K. It used to be advantageous for tax reasons, although that is now much less so. But it enables people to drive cars they would never choose out of their own pockets. So the system continues. I have a car like that, a complete extravagance.

GRAHAM GALER: I would more or less give up on the responsible consumer. Even Kees and myself, ultraresponsible and
ecologically aware as we are, drive bigger cars than we need
to, because the market/fiscal regime we live in makes it
rational to do so. What is to be gained by our behaving in
any way other than with this enlightened self-interest?

However, the responsible consumer can be influenced in
his choices by the responsible corporation, and he wears
another hat as a responsible citizen. Shouldn't the responsible corporation be lobbying, in its own long-term interest,
for fiscal and legislative regimes which are "responsible"?
For instance, in the examples I gave earlier, shouldn't responsible companies in Germany be lobbying for lower
speed limits (instead of making high-speed cars); in the
U.K., for an end to the market-distorting company-car system (instead of exploiting it); and in the U.S., for a high
gasoline tax (surely the U.S. advertising industry is clever
enough to make this sound attractive)?

4

Freedom, Feminism, and Advertising

●

PETER WARSHALL: I think we had better start thinking about freedom and cars. One of the great incentives for cars was women's liberation in the largest sense. Previously confined to the home, the car allowed her to shop, get the kids to school, stop by and chat with friends, drive to the reservoir and space out, have two careers. The greatest acceleration in car driving is not the out-of-date urban-suburban, but the nouveau intersuburban, gridlock. The sixteen- to seventy-year-old woman has escaped the confinement of nostalgic homemaker (except for the poor who cannot afford cars). Freedom is part of consumer demand, and unless other notions of freedom exist, it always will be.

CATHERINE BATESON: I find myself thinking of the sex-symbol cars of twenty-five years ago—and of the woeful idea of sex they represented in a society of erotic primitives. The vehicular equivalent of wham-bam-thank-you-ma'am. How about an ad campaign that emphasizes finesse and staying power—say, a sexy man with graying sideburns, posed with a car that doesn't wear out, in front of a redwood: "We're in for the long haul"?

NANCY RAMSEY: I've been astonished by a number of comments but none startled me more than the note that women's liberation is one of the great incentives for cars. "Liberation" is not about being allowed to shop, get the kids to school, or have two careers—and, if it were, that "liberated" woman you described would hardly have time to drive by for a chat with a friend or a space-out at the local reservoir! "Women's liberation" has taken a lot of bum raps, but this one is right up there.

A correlation between auto use and changing family and work patterns in American society is perhaps closer to what you had in mind?

PETER WARSHALL: Hello, Nancy; perhaps my use of "women's liberation" was too provocative. I do mean changes in women's work patterns and play patterns.

But the history is delightful. At first, cars were open, and men wore goggles and dusted up the horse-and-buggy roads. Car companies advertised "cars for women," which were enclosed, and everyone bought one. The men, of course, said they were doing it for the women. Then electric cars were invented so that "women" (in the advertisements) did not have to crank the motor. As soon as the electric starters were available, they were added to "men's cars—for the women" (according to the ads).

The whole history of the advertising of car improvements in the U.S. (including Volvo's focus on children's safety) has been directed toward "women," meaning American images of women. Men are supposed to be free of the need for ease. Recently, a BMW television ad showed a woman simply putting suntan lotion on her body, with no voice-over. The last few seconds of the ad cut to a suntan-colored sunset with a BMW fading into it.

Furthermore, in Los Angeles in the 1920s, a women's rebellion took place that changed the shape of the city forever. The city tried to prevent cars in the downtown because they were causing gridlock. The local government supplied trolleys and banned cars! Women led a boycott that eventually led to the birth of suburban shopping centers which has evolved into the mall.

This is not to lay blame or anything like that, but to bring the family and the images that women have of themselves into our discussion of corporate life. The values that limit us to talking only about producers, consumers, stockholders, and labor seem very old-fashioned in this kind of discussion. Let's be daring and open the boundaries very wide.

CHUCK HOUSE: I've been on a fifteen-year kick to help our company (Hewlett-Packard) understand the unfolding computer-world future by analogy with the automotive history of the past century. Most people find this quaint, inappropriate, or maddening.

But there are interesting observations: for some reason, 103 manufacturers of cars in England left brakes as an option for twenty-two years, which is analogous to computers under UNIX operating systems having no private or secure communications.

Americans helped Montgomery defeat the vastly superior (in nearly every way) Rommel in North Africa, because they knew how to take sand out of the carburetors and because, in Germany, where the paradigm was chauffeurs, no one had personal mechanical experience.

The twenties represented a major social scandal to

preachers because of "sex in the back seats," which predates the sixties issues that Catherine referenced above.

Ford, of course, was the dominant player in America; Chrysler the engineering leader; and Bully-GM redefined the rules for both into marketing tastes for Caspar Milquetoast, if not Joe and Sue Six-Pack.

Daimler "cheated" on VW in the early seventies, betting that a campaign for large, glitzy, upscale machines could be made to look socially responsible if diesels were included. Net result was a tenfold—yes, an order of magnitude—switch in the relative fortunes of the two companies. This exactly mapped onto the first gas crisis.

5

Hot Buttons

●

DANICA REMY: I did go out and buy a used 1987 Saab Turbo four months ago. . . .

We could have bought one of any number of cars, but my common sense said, "Why spend the money that could be for a down payment for a house on a car"? A majority of the other [members of my car club] are the same way: one practical car and one not so practical car. My criteria for purchasing a car are:

1) safety (so we considered Saabs, Volvos, Mercedeses, and Rovers);
2) performance;
3) comfort. (Comfort in my book is rated by how the seats hold you while going through the curves, how easy the instruments are to reach when needed, comfort during long drives: i.e., seat, ease getting in and out, and, finally, the road noise.)

Many members of the Classic Sports Racing Group (CSRG) share a similar philosophy: have a car to drive for day-to-day living, and have one to really have fun in. I have two Austin-Healeys (a 1964 AH 3000 purchased twelve years ago and a 1967 AH 3000 purchased three years ago) that come out to play when the weather is nice and when I don't have anything important to do. My first Healey is about to undergo restoration so it can be raced.

It might be interesting to see what the car of choice is for the CSRG and other groups. Something I've noticed is that a lot of the people who race, even as a hobby, have helped make decisions for their friends, since they are perceived as knowing something more about cars.

JACK HUBER: My bride and I left behind a 1959 Austin-Healey when we moved to Greenwich Village for the trip of the sixties. . . . Only walking compares with the Healey.

DANICA REMY: Healey-lovers unite!

JACK HUBER: Yeah! A 100-6, 128-bhp, on 2050 pounds, tight curves, high rpm's and four-wheel drifts. Now Responsibility is looking over my shoulder. Oh, well, I still have my blues-harp!

DANICA REMY: When you're up here in San Francisco, drop by for a spin in my 3000, Jack!

JACK HUBER: Danica—you're on!

PETER GLEICK: Doesn't this "automobile-love/fixation" bother anyone else? No offense, Danica and Jack, but I find it hard to think of the automobile in positive terms at all. I accept the need for toys and play, but I also can't escape the larger ramifications of CARS.

JIM PELKEY: I am in the camp of cars-as-a-necessary-fixture. Owned Toyotas for years and couldn't have been more happy—ran them until they dropped. Now I have to drive a big hog Cadillac for medical reasons, and it is poorly made and is plainly a piece of junk. Having just moved to

Santa Fe, New Mexico, I also bought a Jeep for the winter, because we live two miles down a dirt road that deteriorates rapidly with rain.

PETER SCHWARTZ: I own a 1971 BMW 3.0 CS that I have recently put into storage, despite an enduring passion. The emissions were getting worse. Selling it would have kept it on the road, and I do get to visit it now and then, fondle its leather and wood, and admire its lines, but no more clouds of gray smoke from leaded premium gasoline at well under 20 mpg.

Images That Sell

●

STEVE BARNETT: What about today's [7/26/90] New York Times business-section article on the BMW ad-agency idea of "responsibility"?

PAMELA McCORDUCK: I read that with great interest, Steve. And some surprise. Wondered why now? The aging of the baby boomers seems a bit too glib.

STEVE BARNETT: Not only aging baby boomers; BMW is responding to a much broader awareness of the consumer's sense of responsibility. In Europe, BMW is the first auto company to build a recycling plant for its older cars. Clever devils!

PETER SCHWARTZ: The New York Times article about BMW seemed to focus more on how to market BMWs than on what kind of company they should be or what kind of cars they should build. In other words, the selling of "responsibility" rather than being responsible.

STEVE BARNETT: Peter, is selling "being," being "selling"? Does the oh-so-free-market society allow us to differentiate, can the hoi polloi also differentiate? Sizzle vs. steak is an old issue.

I'm a bit glib, but there is a real question here. How does a corp. decide how far to go—to their ad agency or all the way to the ecological web (discussed later under "The Corporation," pp. 93–155)? How can the benefits/liabilities of how far a corporation goes be calculated?

PETER SCHWARTZ: People have a way of knowing what is false and, in a fairly open society with an aggressive press, companies that are mainly rhetoric rather than reality will get caught out.

PETER WARSHALL: God, Steve, to show you where my head is, I read: "How far does a carp decide to go?" Carp are pretty sedentary and I've never really thought of carp migrations. Thanks.

DON MICHAEL: In the Bay Area there is a radio station that broadcasts good classical music exclusively. Currently, it carries ads for its upscale audience that go this way:

For Toyota: A family of four, each driving a new Toyota, is being exposed by the enthusiastic father in the lead vehicle (natch) to the delight of a "Toyota vacation experience" or some such. Much jovial family wisecracking.

In an aerobics class, one young woman is commenting to another that she needs a workout because "she hardly walks anywhere now that she has her new Celica." After a while they become bored and the second says, in effect, "Forget this, let's go ride in your new Celica . . . ," which they do exuberantly.

For Jeep: One upscale guy is telling his pal about the virtues of his four-wheel-drive, super-powered Cherokee. In the background, birds are chirping. Sometimes preceding this ad, sometimes at other times, a woman's voice gives a report on the status of the state's forests. Sponsored by Jeep.

So clients and the agencies must believe there are lots of folks to be favorably influenced by these ads. Presumably, too, they are either ignoring the distrust and disgust such ads might engender in other listeners, or it hasn't occurred to them that such might be the case.

PAMELA McCORDUCK: Or it may be that for most listeners, even those sensitive souls tuned in to KKHI (I listen too, Don, and have heard each of those ads), the clients and agencies are correct. Mostly they/we file it away as adland hyperbole, no more or less offensive than zillions of others. The juxtaposition with state forest reports is just one more media oddment.

DON MICHAEL: Agreed, Pamela, but what gets filed along with the acceptance of adland hyperbole is distrust in whatever the product claims. When we have a society that sees increasing reason to disbelieve whatever it is told by communicators of whatever ilk, while, at the same time, the boundaries are disappearing, what reasons have we to believe in a growth of responsibility re the use of transportation modes? Quite the contrary, I think . . . except for we unhappy few. . . .

7

Winning Public Trust

●

DON MICHAEL: Let us consider some ways in which the next fifteen or twenty years could affect both personal and societal definitions of responsibility, as well as how one should conduct oneself accordingly. These include:

- trust of corporations, government, science, engineering, and one's fellow person;
- crime and personal security;
- values re environmental protection (e.g., jobs vs. endangered species or air quality);
- perceptions of the state of one's experienced environment and perceptions of the state of the reported-on environment (e.g., after another *Valdez* or Chernobyl);
- responses perceived as relevant (by whom?) elsewhere (in the U.S., Europe, and especially Japan).

How would these circumstances color our picture of what should or may in fact be the interplay among producers and consumers of the automobile and its technology?

PETER SCHWARTZ: Does scale have something to do with our inherent mistrust of big companies such as car manufacturers? Like big government, big business seems essentially unaccountable to me as an individual, whereas my local dry cleaner tries real hard for his neighbor, even if he's misplaced his receipt. Is our sense that large companies are irresponsible in fact an almost unconscious mistrust of size in all forms?

STEWART BRAND: Peter, I think that's an accurate perception by people, that huge firms are largely focused on themselves. Maybe a way to deal with that is for huge firms to take on environmental problems that are huge in scale, so you get a scale matching that makes sense to people and that might make sense in terms of problem solving.

DOUG CARMICHAEL: Having consulted in the last few years for AT&T, I've been struck by how the desire for autonomy and control is so powerful that talented managers opt for a product which they can isolate, rather than aligning their careers with large systems. In fact, the large system potentially seems to have no constituency; people think of AT&T as an ensemble of small companies that can no longer afford the overhead of the front office and would like to do without it.

PAMELA McCORDUCK: Are you saying that corporations with the wherewithal to take on large-scale environmental problems simply won't because no corporate champion (a necessary agent for getting things done) will come forward to take on such an amorphous responsibility (that word again!)?

DOUG CARMICHAEL: Pamela, yes, but I think the Japanese more easily enjoy thinking about these larger meta-issues in which the large corporation is a potential player.

BARBARA HEINZEN: Possibly, but it is my impression that Japanese corporations are more likely to work for the commonweal when some higher authority is saying, "DO THIS!" to all participants, so that no one loses any competitive edge, whether from the cost of initiating action or that of abstaining from it.

STEVE BARNETT: Don't smaller entities (like your local dry cleaner) get off too easily? Sure, they're personally nice, but what chemicals do they use? Do they know? A major car company has to be aware of many thousands of such issues, yet really can't expect credit for handling each minute concern.

PAMELA McCORDUCK: In the case of the dry cleaner, the enterprise is regulated, sometimes even monitored, by local authorities. If it somehow still manages to break the law (dump harmful chemicals), then the landlord is responsible. If you try to sell a property where a dry cleaner is or has been, you must prove that it has behaved itself, else pay for the cleanup yourself, before you can sell.

PETER COYOTE: I am confused as to the hierarchy of values implied by "responsibility." Are we responsible first to the species, human comfort, good business, the health of the planet, or what? I opt for long-term habitation of the planet as the best mechanism for affording us the time to sort out the other diddly. So until we agree about what we want or consider optimum, or what the spectrum of such possibilities is, I don't understand what we are speaking about.

A corporation, as I understand it, is responsible to its stockholders. It considers the community, the culture, et al., as the source of revenue that eventually supplies wealth to those stockholders. It makes calculated risks, like Ford deciding that it was cheaper to pay off deaths caused by design flaws in the Pinto than retooling the whole line to correct the flaws.

PETER WARSHALL: Frankly, with cars, I am not sure what I want. I mean, I use vehicles all the time to get places I'd rather walk to, because walking from my house is a stroll on Speedway. "To get away" becomes an important concept if you have a car. I'd rather get the gridlock out of the city and make it more livable, sociable, and fun. Peter Coyote and I met after many years, in a Paris café.

PETER SCHWARTZ: For me the concept of responsibility has to do with a sense of obligation which encompasses both liability and a positive, creative need to make things better. I often feel that in some companies the social milieu is a sense of mutual obligation, while in others there is a sense of mutual victimization. I have no obligation to someone who is victimizing me.

ELSA PORTER: I'd like to talk about the connections that I am seeing and experiencing between cars and one's proverbial castle. Here in northern Virginia, just outside of Washington, D.C., we are running out of living room. But people keep pouring in and houses keep getting built within a wider and wider perimeter. The people who moved to the country are now faced not only with "development" but also with major interstate highway bypasses that threaten to turn their rural estates into clover-leaf exchanges. They have understandably blocked the construction of both eastern and western bypasses for north-south traffic which comes up I-95 past my town of Alexandria, in fact right by my window overlooking the Woodrow Wilson Bridge and the Potomac River.

So we are faced with gridlock here—and the political decision proposed is to more than double the size of the bridge, to fourteen lanes, knocking down my condo or my neighbor's to make room for what will resemble the New Jersey Turnpike as one nears New York City.

Naturally, we are fighting this, to protect and preserve our castles. But ours is not the only flashpoint around here. Wherever new housing is being built, those who were there first are taking aim at traffic problems they foresee. A new organization has just been formed, called "NO GRIDLOCK!" made up of citizen volunteers who have pledged to storm city hall if the developers fail to cut down on expected traffic.

None of us, however, has given up our individual car or cars. We need at least one to get from here to there. And so we are in a stalemate that appears to have no political solution. The bridge expansion will not be allowed to happen. People are cheerfully planning to stop it at every step along the way.

A tunnel would please almost everyone except the Congress, which would have to appropriate the money, and the taxpayers across the country, who would foot the bill. Several small tunnels across the river would seem even a better idea, or other novelties, such as fast ferries using the Potomac as a highway.

The point of this long recitation is to suggest that R [responsible] companies need to figure out how to help break the stalemate. Why not invest in R&D to improve tunnel technology so the surface areas are not paved over?

We've reached the point in this area where people are trying to protect their homes against encroaching traffic. An R company would understand its stake in this system over the long haul and would help to invent some solutions.

3
1

8

The Changing Corporate-Customer Relationship

●

DON MICHAEL: Are the majority's beliefs, values, and behaviors likely to become more congruent with ours over fifteen to twenty years or less so—and under the impacts of what?

What might be the consequences for our concerns herein if the division widens—or if it narrows? We know protecting the environment is high on opinion surveys but we also know opinions change. We know lots of books are sold re protecting the environment, etc., but we also know many bought books are never read, or if read are not acted on, or if acted on, then only for a short time. (Look at the decline in safe-sex practice in the gay community or at the small percentage of people who persist in physical exercise.)

What other "measures" need to be watched and evaluated to sense better the future interplay between producers and consumers of automobiles as these are affected by differing patterns of expected and practiced responsibility over the next fifteen to twenty years?

PETER WARSHALL: I remember Ronald Reagan in California

stopping the Eel River dam after the California legislatu..
passed it, because, he said, it would drown the private property of hard-working ranchers. Jerry Brown lost his battle to
save the Stanislaus, in part, because he said on TV that it
was environmentally damaging, and made a big deal of it.

From the action point of view, Reagan played California
better, using the "private property" argument and antago-
nizing the environmentalists, while also handing them what
they wanted. Brown, a purist, eventually shot himself in the
foot.

This "political parable" has to do with cultural "norms";
the art of navigating real-world politics and the strange
twists of fate; and trying to define responsibility before we
know the consequences. That's why a good sense of humor
is crucial. See Ed Abbey or Mark Twain ("There are only
two things that shouldn't be seen in the making: sausage
and law.") From an emotional point of view, certain questions become so heavy that citizens opt for fundamental-
ism. This is the state of the world right now on questions of
"When does life start and what responsibility do we have
for it?" and "When is death and what responsibility do we
have for it?"

Citizens in Christian and Islamic contexts simply go for
the most simple-minded views in many cases. But so do
medical doctors in Africa who feel they should do everything to reduce childhood mortality. The kids in Kenya
grow up, and now the family size is six or seven, and they
can't live off the land, so some kids go to the cities—Nai-
robi is a Dickensian *Bleak House* nightmare (tourists never
see it)—and become alienated and rebel. They die as teen-
agers instead of infants, but the medical doctors (as narrow-
focused as fundamentalists) do not feel any responsibility

for the consequences of their acts or the whole life cycle of the human.

Can you imagine Africa if doctors remained responsible for the life of each child whom they saved between birth and five years? Or antiabortionists agreeing to adopt any unwanted child and care for it with their own money until it was self-sufficient? This is a time when ethics are being stirred up, and the future could be frightening if the boundaries are not peacefully redefined.

STEWART BRAND: Peter, your riff about African babies reminds me that one of the fundamentals we have to keep coming back to is "life-cycle economics"—whether it's a baby, a car, a building (where the term cut deep in energy-use analysis), or a community.

KEVIN KELLY: Are there any working parts of "life-cycle economics"? Or is this a goal?

CATHERINE BATESON: Kevin, it is idiotic to base market strategies on adolescence, which is both committed to the totally transient and feels it is immortal. The human challenge is to go on living, contingently, tenuously, and not forever.

STEWART BRAND: Aha! Catherine, I hadn't before connected product "life-cycle accounting" with human individual "life-cycle accounting."

This raises the notion of "maturity" in products and companies. It also questions whether some customers have outgrown the attraction of supplier-as-parent.

PAMELA McCORDUCK: Products for the mature adult . . . Stewart, could you elaborate on what you mean by outgrowing the attraction of supplier-as-parent? Are you saying that a supplier (or corporation) is regarded by the immature as in loco parentis, that it will pick up after you, stay up late for you, love you even when you aren't lovable, and so forth?

CATHERINE BATESON: Earlier, I made a rather tongue-in-cheek proposal for marketing cars based on mature rather than adolescent sexuality. It was based on my sense that there has been a real change in the level of understanding of adult sexuality so that people are not caught in models that begin with energy to burn, dogged by a fear of inevitable failure. It seemed to me that we were due for an extension of the new understanding of skill (and patience) in lovemaking to other areas. Sustainability rather than flash.

Parenthetically, I put my daughter on a clothing allowance when she was about ten and she has become extremely conscious of not buying things that don't last.

I'm with Pamela in finding the supplier-as-Momma interesting but puzzling. It doesn't ring any immediate bell for me, but it feels like imagery that's very important to explore.

STEWART BRAND: Remember "Ma Bell"? And how we all whined and threw tantrums when we had to make our own decisions about telephone hardware and services after divestiture?

It's fun thinking of some companies as parent substitutes. It's easy to see why they adopt the practice—since there are such prodigious rents attainable if you fill your customer's life and have complete trusted say-so.

IBM is the stern, benevolent parent. You can play with PCs, if you must, but be sure to stay connected (via their e-mail system) to the mainframe or mini you've trusted for so long. When you catch on to the insidious dependency game, IBM is deeply disappointed in you, warning regretfully about the terrible things that will happen to you out there in the mean streets.

Apple was the really neat older brother, full of adventure and cool ideas, but then he got married and predictable. You keep up the old badinage with him, but the awestruck admiration is gone. My shift of loyalty from L. L. Bean to Patagonia was the shift from an honest, chuckling grandpa (who turned out to be just chuckling) to relations with a peer, which does honor to both of us.

KEVIN KELLY: There are (at least) two life cycles circulating here: the passage of surrogate parent companies and the passage of customers (who mature as, say, boomers age, for instance) and markets (which evolve regardless of the boomers' age, by way of more information and higher expectations). I suspect there are other life cycles (the passage and evolution of the notion of surrogate parents itself) if we looked for them.

9

Who Buys What

●

CHUCK HOUSE: My dad bought cars to drive them. So did my wife's father. They each drive some now, but during one part of their lives it was 100K miles per year.

Selling sausage to small-town grocers or stell-plate to blacksmith shops is a lot of driving. Still, I learned somehow to buy cars for their safety (probably because my driving scared me). So my first car was a '56 Ford new, because of their safety steering wheel and cushioned dash and visors. That year, Chevy creamed 'em in the marketplace, and they dropped the safety campaign.

I bought a '65 VW in '64 which still is parked in front of my ex-wife's home, and taught all my children to drive in it (it served as the school car for all through college for each but the last). Then Volvo did the great safety-144, and I bought one which went 137K miles for me; then one night it did its collapsible notion, saving the life of a woman who worked for us.

My first Japanese car was a Nissan pickup in 1970, called

S Datsun then, which was strange to my dad and virtually all my Colorado neighbors. We took off the rear section, mounted a flatbed with stake sides, and used it as the best floral/nursery truck for years. Looked around one day and found I owned six cars and trucks. All useful; one, a Porsche, was for mid-life-crisis fun. Sold it because of high rate of ticket acquisition and its ability to promote unsafe driving and living practices in me.

Moved to Palo Alto, walk to most things I enjoy with my wife and our two dogs. We own a '90 Acura for her to go to work two days a week. The rest of her time is with a Super-Shuttle or limo to/from San Francisco airport.

"My" car is supplied by Hewlett-Packard, as it has been for seventeen years. I get a new one each year, I drive it to some HP location from Roseville or Santa Rosa to San Jose twice a week, usually to Sunnyvale twenty miles away—and one day a week to San Francisco or San Jose airport to rent a car in Colorado, and two days a week to other parts of the country to rent two to four cars that week. Or be picked up, or take other forms of transport. Still love cars, however. Driving four hundred miles a day is "a piece of cake" and driving 150 mph is still a thrill. Hardly ecological.

STEWART BRAND: I walk two hundred yards to work, and love it. Problematic side effect—I drive so little that, when I do, it sometimes scares me: all that hurtling metal!

ELSA PORTER: Are any of you regular listeners of "Car Talk" on National Public Radio? These two brothers in New York take calls from people all over the country asking about what cars to buy, how to fix things, what symptoms of trouble are related to which problems, etc.

Last Saturday I caught the program when they were giving advice to a young couple with child about the best buy for safety, reliability, comfort, design, etc. I learned that the no. 1 yuppy choice these days is the Isuzu Trooper. (My daughter, husband, and baby have one. I didn't know it was The Car.) In our day, with young kids, we had a big, hunky station wagon—middle-class Ford or Chevy. For understanding cultural, personal, generational, etc., reasons for choosing a car, these guys are experts—and fun to hear.

DOUG CARMICHAEL: Is the Trooper craze (and other Jeep look-alikes) part of getting our kids ready for the war computer games have already skilled them for?

STEWART BRAND: Such cars are like the running shoes that no one runs in—abstract consumerism, or outfitting your fantasy. Four-wheel-drive Jeeplike cars are also popular in Japan, which has almost no place to exercise them. So there are commercial places you can hire to go bounce around in four-wheel drive.

10

The Rewards of a Good Reputation

●

DON MICHAEL: In "Convenience and Freedom," p. 74, Barbara Heinzen said: "The mall is the epitome of automobile-designed commerce but lacks all the vitality and quirkiness of a centralized street market. It also promotes capital-intensive trading rather than labor-intensive trading and probably expands the gap between the haves and have-nots.

"Which leads us into a much broader systemic consideration of responsibility and a need to ask: Whose interests do we want to serve first?"

Apropos her observation, consider this: in St. Louis now, Chrysler is going to close a plant. Many people will lose jobs and income directly and indirectly. Members of the St. Louis community are insisting that, since Chrysler was put back on its feet by public monies, it has a responsibility to the community to get it back on its feet, if and when the plant is closed.

Boundary loss between public and private; "broader systemic consideration"; responsibility?

ART KLEINER: Does an auto company have responsibility for dealing with gridlock? Does it have more responsibility for air pollution than for gridlock? Or is it just that the air-quality problem is perceived as more severe?

Does it have more responsibility for highway safety than for air pollution?

Is there a limit to a company's ability to take on social responsibility? As auto companies take on responsibility for air pollution, does that mean they pay less attention to highway safety? Or is safety "solved," so that it no longer needs to be a matter for concern?

Where does legitimate social responsibility end and lobbying for special interests begin (in practice)?

STEVE BARNETT: The middle seems to be dropping out—either companies need to have cosmic responsibility or none. What about genuine concern (execs also are afraid of eco-doom and terminal quotidian-banality) which is in real life constrained by making money, competing (thus limiting corporate cooperation in "fixing" auto-related issues), satisfying diverse constituencies, developing an appropriate adversarial relation to government, etc. Do these factors hedge matters so much that corporate responsibility becomes meaningless?

Ignoring the pseudoreligious wish for the just-in-time techno-fix that saves us by, say, eliminating the engine, gridlock, or whatever, can a company be incremental—doing what it can, more than other companies, but not much more? Does this sound too boring, given present conundrums? Can a company do more in a capitalist framework? Do we bag capitalism as well as socialism?

Norman Mailer, no political hero of mine, said when asked what he thought about capitalism and socialism (running for N.Y. mayor, remember that?), "A plague on both their houses."

PETER SCHWARTZ: The middle of the road rarely wins much strong commitment, but the friendly-old-dog quality of middle-of-the-road George Bush seems to be winning a surprisingly large percentage of Americans over. Perhaps there is a way to be incremental without being inadequate?

ART KLEINER: One possibility is that being responsible might become a source of competitive advantage. It's easier to see this in the chemical industry, where "homeopathic" attitudes could change practices, than in the auto industry.

It's possible, for instance, that a tiny amount of pesticide could be as effective as a large amount—and that a chemical company could prosper by selling the small amount, along with its expertise in applying it, for nearly the same amount of money that it previously charged for the large amount. Moreover, the higher level of expertise (and of complying with regulations) would now become a cost of entering the chemical business.

But you can't sell "part" of a car.

PETER WARSHALL: I think that all the comments about "incremental" and "quantifiable" are truly the heart of responsibility. They are not sexy, though, and a good topic would be how to make incremental or sober judgments and remain sexy!

We see this in the timber business, which refuses to restructure (which would provide for more jobs), and the environmentalists who, not understanding the nature of corporate restructuring, trade structuring, trade barriers, raw logs vs. finished products, cannot get at the economic heart of the problem. Responsibility has turned into a shoot-out.

STEVE BARNETT: Peter, sober-vs.-sexy matters in corporate life. If most companies in a sector like cars are claiming to be responsible, how the hell can anyone, especially consumers, figure which company, if any, really is responsible? It might be a shoot-out where no one is hurt, or where everyone dies.

Even if too trendy, Baudrillard is rightish that only the surface counts in the contemporary U.S., but then does accountability itself also become a paper-thin illusion?

PAMELA McCORDUCK: Luckily, Baudrillard isn't right about that (or much of anything else).

PETER WARSHALL: Despite jibes at Baudrillard, he brings the question of images, and how they can be used, to the surface (see "What Do Consumers Believe?" p. 53).

PAMELA McCORDUCK: Surely most people put their own immediate concerns first (safety, economy, in the case of some; zippiness, style, in the case of others), and a car's effect on the environment lags way out there. Not Earth First!

Thus, I suspect the responsible car maker would have to address those immediate concerns and add environmental R as lagniappe. I think you could even make plausible arguments that self-interest for an individual is a responsible stance. But things aren't either/or. My grocery is selling nontoxified veggies that were once available only in health food stores. Customer self-interest? Yes. Customer education? Yes. Good for the earth? Yes.

PETER SCHWARTZ: Pamela, I think more and more people believe that improving the environment is in their self-interest now, not just in the interest of the spotted owl. . . . And this is a new phenomenon.

KEVIN KELLY: Pamela, your comments about self-interest are spot on. If I were shopping for a car, environmental concerns would be on the list, but not at the top. My list might go: Price, Performance, Safety, Reliability, Environment.

In an interesting sense, I consider gasoline mileage figures to be part of price and performance, rather than environmental. What this list in fact means is that, all other factors being equal, I'd take the R-car. But what price or what performance-cost would I trade off for R-ness? I don't know. How much safety would I trade for R-ness? Probably none at all.

For some products, like food, my self-interest in the product's R-ness is high. I'll even put R above price. But in that sense, R-ness is just a variety of safety, much as if a car were to leak gas fumes or carbon monoxide.

But how does one come to see the origins of the car's bodywork, for instance, in a self-interested way? How does one make miles-per-gallon into a "safety" issue? Primarily by education.

But I have to work at it. My guess is that the quickest way to bring environmental factors out of the basement is to incorporate them into the other factors that are closer to selfishness—to make R-ness more a cofactor in terms of price, safety, and performance.

4
4

What Business Are We In?

●

KEES VAN DER HEIJDEN: It seems to me that few companies that have been in business for more than ten years really know what they are selling. Therefore all companies interested in their survival need to engage in "concept research" from time to time. This is basically an exercise in reframing, in which you think through the limitations imposed by a boundary between your system and another system, by carrying out the thought experiment of imagining the two as one.

If you do that with the car company and its customers. I am not so sure that you end up with "the transportation business." What we see happening between these two reveals that there is a lot more going on than transportation. Why do people sit in gridlocks for hours? Why do they do this in the most expensive vehicle they can afford? Why do people love to drive? What is the role of status, what is the role of freedom, etc.?

And maybe the car-company/car-buyer system is too

small. Maybe we should include in our thought experiment some other constituents, even including the same people in another scenario, e.g., if they have to get somewhere fast.

PETER WARSHALL: Let's start from the language—"responsible" has the "re" part, which means once again, back, feedback. There's also "spond," which suggests making an offering, performing a rite, hence engaging oneself in a ritual act. It's also found in words like "sponsor," "spouse," "respond" (to make a solemn promise, pledge, betroth), and "spondee" (a libation, offering).

THIS IS SERIOUS STUFF. In Acoma, the Pueblo hunters go through sweat baths, give pollen libations, wish the deer good luck in its journey to the world of souls, and pray that it has been treated well in its death and will return to be hunted once more.

Since we have psychobabbled ritual and believe the coach is more useful than the spondee, we might note that cars are the essence of American ritual—from *Rebel Without a Cause* to the all-inclusive-entertainment/communication (have a fax in your car while you wait at the toll booth) BMW. We are asking a lot to have business start dealing (as Steve Barnett is) with imagery, symbols, meta-language, subliminal advertising, and what street people more crudely call mind fucking.

Yet responsibility in its very essence includes a commitment or pledge.

Synonyms for responsibility include answerable, accountable, liable, and amenable. To help, we might say: Whose care or welfare is the corporation legally or ethically accountable to? Or, can the corporation be trusted or depended upon, be reliable? (Good-bye, Perrier!) Do they have "good" judgment or "sound" thinking? (Good-bye,

Exxon! But, still with you, Volvo.) These questions can also be posed to individuals in business.

PAMELA McCORDUCK: I proposed elsewhere that the nomination of David Souter to the Supreme Court might signal the return to principle and abstemiousness, qualities that, believe it or not, folks, are deep in the Yankee grain. Does anyone else remember "Make do, make it last, or do without"?

However, we are a pluralistic society and elected Ronald Reagan as our President twice. And we have an alarming tendency to confuse surface with substance, I agree.

BARBARA HEINZEN: I agree about David Souter. In a sense, this is arguing that the way he arrives at decisions is more important than the particular decisions he makes. It is also a shrewd political move, since it sidesteps all the issues that have cluttered the surface of debate.

STEWART BRAND: Barbara, the clause, "the way he arrives at decisions is more important than the particular decisions," may be a major part of how a business is responsible and looks responsible. Question: Are businesses willing to offer up some transparency in how such decisions are arrived at? Traditionally, they are not. That might be one of the changes necessary.

RUSTY SCHWEICKART: The "way decisions are (really) made" is a pretty tough domain in which to gain visibility! I don't know why and how I really make decisions. How in blazes would anyone build their confidence in Responsible Meats by watching closely their decision making re sausage production? If I were the CEO, I wouldn't bet the company on it!

KEVIN KELLY: Let's say, for the sake of this argument, that the most "responsible car" one could make right now were made of 95% polystyrene, ran on rare-earth batteries, and was covered head to toe with photovoltaic cells. But let's say few people really saw this as "responsible" ("All that plastic!"), or agreed on the limits of use it imposed (maximum mileage per charge-up, 500 miles), or even wanted to buy it ("It's got WARTS!"). So R-Car, Inc., which only makes nature-safe R-cars, doesn't sell any cars. Soon R-Car is dead, and there are no R-cars.

Or it might be that the R-car we just designed today as the most R will turn out to be very anti-R because of new scientific evidence published a year after it comes on the market. By the same token, a car from the past may now be seen as more R than was first realized, because of the increase in our knowledge. The R of a car is thus to some degree a measure of appropriateness, a measure that shifts, and one that is assigned by consensus (as Kees has argued). Unless such appropriateness is perceived by society (or at least some of it), any R-car will die, even if it turns out in retrospect to be more R than society perceived it to be.

The R-car therefore can't really exist outside of the perceptions of the public. It's a ruse, an advertising gimmick: "This Year's Responsible Car." Nobody can guarantee that their car is the most responsible or appropriate, because it all shifts and is pretty relative to how you use the car and to what else is known about the world. But you can have a responsible car company that has a contract or relationship or communication with you, and which will, in short, respond to you, unlike a car, which is fixed and inanimate. The cars that the R-Car Company makes are not R. But the R-Car Company itself becomes responsible by: (a) giving you a car that meets *your* expectation of appropriateness, thus maintaining a relationship with you, so that (b) if your awareness of appropriateness or responsibility does change, they will know, or (c) if their awareness of appropriateness or responsibility changes, you will know.

I think the major shift in corporate ideas about responsibility must be to understand that the customer is part of the company. Just as there has been great awareness of the importance of interoffice communication in big companies, the next step is to extend that circle out to the customer. When the customer becomes a working part of the company, then responsibility can flow easily. Lip service won't do this, which is why smaller companies often beat out mammoth ones—they really can figure the customer as part of the organization, and not just the object outside.

I think the design of an ideal, actual, you-can-buy, R-car can only come from a responsible car company, because there has to be an organism like that, one that is capable of holding responsibility and adapting it. What the design actually is hardly matters right now, in part because there will not be one but many.

STEWART BRAND: Rusty, Kevin's scheme of involving the customer more intimately and conspicuously in the perpetual redesign process is exactly what I mean by a more transparent decision process. I agree that publishing transcripts of design-team wrangles or board vendettas would be vile for all concerned. But if, for example, Ralph Nader were known to have participated in the discussion leading to the current model, and he expressed publicly some satisfaction that his ideas and viewpoints were heeded, that would open a window into the decision process that might serve everybody.

You'd take the chance, of course, that Ralph Nader or his equivalent would seize the opportunity to fire a now well-informed blaze of cheap shots in your direction or to reveal the actual arbitrariness of the design process, if that's what happened.

Transparency takes a lot of trust, but it inspires trust in turn like nothing else. *Whole Earth* has been publishing its financial accounts in excruciating detail since its first day, and has been rewarded for that every day since. It hurts sometimes, but it is hugely worth it.

CATHERINE BATESON: I think that the discussion of transparency and of attitudes toward the customer proposes an interesting distinction between responsibility and responsiveness. I'd like to combine that with a restatement of something I said earlier about offering choices. There are a lot of risks in going around telling corporations or consumers that they ought to be responsible, not the least of which is losing money. One gets rapidly into a paternalistic guilt-tripping mode. The R-car is not the product of a set of norms but of a dialogue. The R-car company makes not one model (why do we seem to assume that?) but several, and probably has a considerable customizing capacity like Volvo. Some of these models may lose money for a time or pay off primarily in image and in R&R and the development of capacity to switch to a new kind of product as demand develops—the R model might be a loss leader for a considerable period but is also insurance for the corporation.

On the other hand, the initiation of dialogue involves a new degree of respect for the consumer and the possibility of working toward a product that is seen as both R and desirable. Instead, many corporations are positioned so that growing discrimination and ecological awareness on the part of consumers would spell their doom, a hell of a position to be in. So the R company positions itself to benefit from the R consumer; gets ahead of regulation; educates and dialogues with the consumer. And, realistically, makes money in the meantime.

Might the same model apply to the media? Low-quality network TV may come from negative assumptions about consumers—giving them what they "want" by assuming that they prefer junk and that anything of quality must taste like medicine and "be good for you." Paternalism/snobbery/disdain in the same package.

BARBARA HEINZEN: I like the idea of a dialogue which educates both the customer and the corporation. What you are then saying, possibly, is that the responsible company offers a way of learning and moving forward together.

CATHERINE BATESON: Barbara, yes—conversations, not answers.

ART KLEINER: Some direct experiences, as a reporter covering corporations, about transparency. Most corporate people whom I talk to do not seem to have a clear idea of what they can and cannot say. Some are rigidly controlled by the public relations person, who will go and sit there during the interview. Most are on their own (blessedly), convinced that talking to reporters is a good thing. There is always a dance about how much can be said. I always promise to check quotes and facts before publication, and nearly always do; but I always find myself fretting, even so, about whether I'm putting a spin on my story that will hurt a person. Usually, I'm not. But I've been given very few clues about where the line should be drawn.

Ostensibly, the argument is competitive advantage. Any secret that *should* (rather, *could*) be secret *should* be secret.

Dow Chemical went through a change of heart during the 1980s which I am still researching. It had to do with

51

environmentalism. Their practices did change some (to what extent is a subject for disagreement among observers I've talked to who are from government and environmental groups). Their *openness* changed dramatically—this is the single most tangible thing to point to. In 1978 they were suing the EPA for flying planes overhead trying to measure smokestacks. In 1986 they were inviting environmental groups to sit in on design meetings for a new plant they were building—exactly the sort of design transparency that Stewart and Kevin talk about above.

Remarks made about trust are exactly to the point. Dow's "Great Things" advertising campaigns in which (for instance) we learn from hikers in the Sierra that polystyrene can be recycled (into park benches, not into more clamshell fast-food containers) are not in the same league as their design openness. They're trying to emulate the openness with an advertising slickness. In the process, the ad reveals the mistrust that they still seem to feel, mistrust of consumers, I guess. Mistrust of *our* trust of them.

KEES VAN DER HEIJDEN: The last several comments contain some fundamental advice to any company that, if heeded, could be worth millions and assure survival. They are good examples of the "concept research" which I suggested earlier that the Responsible (or any other) Company should engage in.

Could I suggest one further step? In this conversation with your customer, you will need to acknowledge that the optimum product is a package involving other suppliers who are better than you in some aspects of the ultimate R-product/R-service. So, besides customers, also make other suppliers a part of your system.

12

What Do Consumers Believe?

●

PETER WARSHALL: It is after 1984, images can reflect (as in old-fashioned metaphor), cover up, misdirect, create fluff on top of fluff (referring to the first fluff as "real"), confuse and baffle, con, even kill. The borderline between advertising and simulating reality in "evil" ways is not always clear.

I would like to hear more from you on what you think reasonable images in car advertising might contain. What are the limits within Nissan? For instance, there is an ad that compares Chrysler to Honda owners (I think; I have no TV) that says Chrysler owners find their cars blah-blah times preferable to Hondas. For one second, a subtitle reads, "From a survey of Chrysler owners." Is this "responsible" advertising for Nissan? How is the "ethics" of ads debated?

ART KLEINER: The best watchdogs on that sort of advertising are competitors. If Honda—I mean, if Chrysler—couldn't back up its claims somehow, then Honda could file a complaint with the Federal Trade Commission. I heard in 1987—

88 that the FTC, despite seven years of Reaganism then, had a reputation for close enforcement of misleading advertising rules.

Michael Shudson wrote that advertising is "capitalism's way of saying 'I love you' to itself." In that sense, it maybe doesn't matter what the content of the ad says, as long as the name is spelled right. Public relations on the other hand, I think, matters a great deal, but as a vehicle for helping companies know what their public thinks of them.

STEVE BARNETT: The ethics of ads are intensely debated (Is it responsible to emphasize performance as Nissan currently does, for example?), but there is no structure to the debate, nor is there any ombudsman to try for the hint of objectivity. A nasty conundrum is: Can we create ads that work as ads (grab the hapless consumer and make him/her buy), yet embody a sense of responsibility?

STEVE BARNETT: We are doing a lot of talking about "the customer" (relations with the company, etc.) and almost no talking about who that customer is. Pardon me, but we are an elite, even though we might want to speak for the masses. What do you (collectively) think the "average" consumer is up to in terms of a sense of responsibility—is it formed/unformed, trendy/enduring, at the level of talk or of action? Is responsibility (I hesitate to try this) a consumer trend? If a company tries to be more R (I'm putting this carefully), will it sell to the likes of some of us, or is there an actual market out there?

BARBARA HEINZEN: Steve, your question on advertising and what about the masses (not the elite) brings me back to Catherine's idea of a dialogue between the corporation and customer. Surely advertising should be used to push environmental ideals which might not otherwise be acceptable; perhaps there is a way of moving from advertising (one-way communication) to dialogue, which should involve interactive learning.

KEES VAN DER HEIJDEN: Those of you who read *The Economist* know that here in the U.K. we have what is called the "Volvo vote." These are the people who vote the middle way, would love to get out of the adversarial Anglo-Saxon idea of right/left politics into a middle area based on compromise and consensus. I do not know why, but these people are, in the public's mind, associated with Volvo. What does that mean?

STEWART BRAND: It means safety over flash, I always assumed. Volvo owners tend to be parents.

BARBARA HEINZEN: Or possibly sufficient self-respect that it is not necessary to win 100% of every argument all of the time.

DOUG CARMICHAEL: Volvo is Swedish. Swedish has a word *logam*, meaning moderation, the middle way, taught to kids from early age. It's deep in the psyche of the Swedes, perhaps enough to communicate across cultural boundaries.

STEWART BRAND: Has there been indication or evidence yet that people are willing to pay more for environmentally finessed gasolines than for the usual mixes?

STEVE BARNETT: What about the news that Chevron and Shell, both making much noise about "cleaner" gasoline, in fact have higher levels of benzene than other companies? Responsibility is a dangerous, easily backfiring word.

KEES VAN DER HEIJDEN: Stewart, most people are both willing

and unwilling to pay for cleaner performance. Willing if it produces results, unwilling if "I am the only one." The old "tragedy of the commons."

STEWART BRAND: Kees, has it been tried lately? I would relish paying somewhat more for a fuel I felt much better about. If it involves retooling hassle, though, or being dependent on that kind of fuel, probably I'd skip it.

and promotes the idea that the way to avoid public attack is a combination of secrecy and stonewalling.

PETER WARSHALL: SAS, when it arrives at decisions, seems to have incorporated some environmental thinking. It is the leader on careful use of deicing chemicals, for instance. It is interested in environmental health problems within the cabin (pilots have high ultraviolet exposure, microbes recirculate endlessly, etc.) Their corporate building is a pleasure (little offices force workers to the more pleasant chatting areas). They cannot be totally responsible as they are a holding company and have odd parts such as duty-free shops that are very vulnerable to claims of "We are a green company." Nevertheless, they continually reevaluate labor, ecological, and health priorities.

STEWART BRAND: I realize, reading some of these comments, how much the perception of responsibility in a company has to do with customer "loyalty." I remember once being almost religiously loyal to L. L. Bean—based on the no-nonsense products and product descriptions, the no-questions return policy, the fact that product prices included delivery cost, the perception of a knowable man responsible (Mr. Bean). Then came word that the Bean organization was strongly and actively supporting a nuclear power plant in New England; the products became more chichi; the company was obviously knocking off (imitating) competing products, after using the competitors' product in the catalog for market testing; and the contents became totally predictable and unremarkable, devoid of "real" reference. I don't even scan the catalog now, and I do scan most catalogs. I feel betrayed. Car companies seem to me to be even more involved in passionate customer loyalty. A related case would be Harley-Davidson's fall from and return to grace. That one is a religion.

KEVIN KELLY: There's that "trust" word again. Amazing thing is that (a) there is no formula for building trust; (b) it must be built over time, it cannot be imported or installed; and (c) there is no guarantee it will be maintained.

Begins to sound like marriage.

PAMELA McCORDUCK: Responsiveness matters in a corporation's dealings with its customers or clients. I like dealing with American Express (which takes me at my word when there's a disputed item) and with Citibank. I'd do almost anything to keep from dealing with my former bank, Chemical Bank; anything, that is, except deal with New York Telephone, which takes the attitude "guilty and no way you can prove you're innocent." Service, in a word.

ART KLEINER: And yet we just had a horrid experience of American Express *not* taking our word. (They disagreed with our bank about whether a check had bounced. In fact, it was a nightmare of *our* being bounced from bank to American Express and back again.) We felt like our old terrific relationship with them had been violated. It would not take many such incidents to change our attitude about American Express entirely.

Misery is built into New York Telephone's bureaucracy. One time I interviewed someone at New York Telephone for a story on 976 numbers. I wanted to call up and get his phone number to say I would be a few minutes late. No one in the company could tell me how to reach one of their own employees by phone!

STEWART BRAND: Looks like we're heading in this discussion toward the other kind of exemplary corporations, the ones that head people's list of irresponsible companies (and the ones that really are but you never hear about them). After the *Valdez* spill, one of the most popular and crowded topics on the entire WELL was called "Punishing Exxon."

KEVIN KELLY: These examples illustrate that trust can be rapidly broken and only built up slowly. Therein lies some of the conservatism of large corporations.

PETER GLEICK: Pretty high on my list of "responsible" corporations recently is Dupont (or at least a group there) that agreed within one day of evidence that chlorofluorocarbons were indeed responsible for the destruction of the ozone layer over the Antarctic, to remove CFCs from production by 1995, and to search for safer substitutes. I acknowledge that they have a financial motive to do so by inventing, producing, and selling the alternative, but they still receive high marks for doing the right thing right away.

PETER COYOTE: I will never forget my gratitude to the Filson company in Seattle, when I called them from SFO en route to the Arctic Circle and needed a new pair of whipcords. They delivered them, cut to length, and with suspender buttons sewed on, at the Seattle airport in time for me to transfer to my Alaska flight. That's service. My first pair, which I couldn't find at the time, is fourteen years old and still serviceable. That's a great company.

CHUCK HOUSE: I'd second Art Kleiner's experience with American Express recently, after years of satisfaction. Unfortunately, integrity of corporations begins with individuals, who at some level both reflect and affect how the company works and is perceived, to some degree independently of its founders, philosophy, etc. I used to give a pretty standard talk on corporate ethics inside Hewlett-Packard, and always I talked about Dave Packard's and Bill Hewlett's personal degree of integrity and to some extent social responsibility.

On one occasion in Waldbrunn, Germany, I gave the talk, and, on tour later, I was shown a new liquid chromatograph, with 8-times improvement in resolution. I saw three screens representing orange juice concentrate samples, one of which had a spike on a known carcinogen component. The engineer and I speculated briefly on how this could be, and then I asked, "Well, what have you done about this information?"

And he instantly responded, "Well, I didn't know what to do, so I told our corporate engineering director. We know that he'll know what to do."

The problem for me was—I was the corporate engineering director, and he had just told me! What we did was contact all three suppliers of orange juice sample, describing our equipment and its new resolution, and inviting them to send new samples since we had three which included an obvious "error." All three came back, "Clean: no problem found." And all three sent new samples, which were in fact clean. The same piece of equipment was responsible for doing in Ben Johnson at the 1988 Olympics, even after repeated demonstrations to all trainers and athletes in the world for eighteen months. The question I pose is: What should I have done? What would you do?

DOUG CARMICHAEL: Send his secretary out to buy some of each from a local store and test them. Did I miss something?

CHUCK HOUSE: The thought process I was using was a bit different—we knew beyond much doubt that we had a guilty party; in fact, that is where the original samples came from. The question really is: Do you go to the Feds, do you get an injunction, do you call the president of the offending company, what do you do if you're pretty sure that this is for real?

JACK HUBER: Monsanto and Shell have been cited as responsibility examples. Others might be those corporations who withdrew advertising for the PGA and the corporate members of Shoal Creek who stayed and worked for the acceptance of the first two black members. Or the Dupont of the seventies, which took environmentalism to heart as a way to eliminate waste, increase efficiency, and seek new markets.

All of these examples seem to be following from the same direction—[companies making decisions for their own benefit].

THE
PRODUCT

1

The Evolve-It-Yourself Product

●

DON MICHAEL: What kinds of buttons and bows do you think Joe and Sue [Six-pack] would like on a responsible car to make it attractive enough to buy?

JACK HUBER: What about cars that evolve over time? Suppose you bought into a concept that evolved over a period of time?

You and the manufacturer agree on certain things you want/ they would produce. You buy in with a substantial up-front cost, but each year or two or three you take it in for rehab: a redesigned modular power-train component one time, new interior another, new bells and whistles. Even changes in the exterior—two fenders one year, bumpers and headlights another. But evolving. The same car with new and improved parts and cradle-to-the-grave maintenance. The old parts are recycled by the manufacturer.

Joe and Sue maintain "the latest" with only incremental cost for each upgrade. The manufacturer has a stable base for production and an incentive to evolve better than the competition.

That also gets at the long-term commitment which is required for responsibility. It gives the manufacturer the edge to make those responsible changes which we might not buy into for the short term.

BARBARA HEINZEN: As someone who does not ever want to own a car, I am at a loss to say what kind of car I prefer. But the idea of something that can be rehabbed and evolved over time could be very appealing. Where it might come unstuck is that one could get bored with it and decide that a total change is what is really required.

JACK HUBER: Barbara, could we have a commodity-like trading arrangement which would allow individuals to trade the.? long-term commitments? They could trade contracts instead of cars. The manufacturer still has a base for long-term responsibility. Perhaps the manufacturers could also trade commitments if their directions changed. But the last might diminish trust, which I believe will be a major component of responsibility.

STEWART BRAND: I dearly love Jack's idea of an evolving car. If I could subscribe to a Nissan that I could improve incrementally for the next ten years, I'd do it right now. And talk about building customer loyalty . . . Of course, you would get interesting third-party offerings.

CATHERINE BATESON: I, too, like Huber's evolving car. Let me contextualize it a bit. We have for some time acted as if the "life" of a product were from acquisition to discard—maybe five years for a car, five minutes for a Coke bottle. For a manufacturer, perhaps from time of extraction of materials to end of warranty. It is as if we had forgotten the conservation of matter—all those materials continue to exist—the entropy involved in removing them from pockets of ore, etc., and scattering—and the added modern dynamic of locking them into new compounds that are virtually eternal. Our whole concept of "things" and what happens to them is off key.

Gregory, my father, used to talk about perceiving only arcs of natural cycles (and perceiving them as if lineal). What we need to do is to absorb all of our transactions with the environment into a sense of the biological:

Step 1 involves recycling and biodegradability.

Step 2 involves a kind of assimilation to the human life cycle, with a capacity to heal/be healed, i.e., repair and maintenance.

Step 3 involves artifacts that evolve.

Now, the person who has been thinking about this is Stewart, in relation to buildings. There we have the long-term investment; the realization that they don't just go away when you're through with them; and a lot of experience in rehabbing and retrofitting. Now, people and families do get tired of houses, but they don't generally discard them. It takes a lot of abuse to turn a building into garbage. But we could look at things like rent control that tend to do just that . . . and at mortgage structures that, unlike the rest of our debt structure, may promote maintenance and longer-term thinking . . . because homeownership is effectively a form of savings which promotes a sense of concern for community (even if often manifested as "Not In My Back Yard" thinking, still an aspect of something useful).

Parenthetically, it's no use trying to think biologically about things if in fact we think less and less biologically about human beings. . . .

6
9

STEWART BRAND: Catherine, in recent years the housing market has been modeled more on how people treat cars—trade up. Instead of sticking with the old homestead and adapting it, the market-leader buyers (or successful sellers) move into highly specified homes. With your $40,000 income and two kids, there is an entire housing development calibrated just for you. If you get divorced or change income, then you move to a different place appropriate for that. The mortgage is part of the fungibility.

Some very brittle houses are the result. Like cars. There are some signs this era may be passing for homeowners.

KEVIN KELLY: Stewart, all my contractor friends are reporting a surge of business in the last two years (East Coast) and this year (West Coast). Their theory: people can't afford to trade up, so they are modifying, remodeling, adding on—evolving up, so to speak.

Has anyone noticed how rarely we seem to customize cars? It seems to me hot-rodding is even less prevalent these days, perhaps because cars in the last decade are simply harder to modify. There is also a weird social taboo against modifying your car. Think what reactions there are to a car that is not shiny, or not a solid color, or that's been tinkered with in any substantial way. There is not the same reaction to the same done to a house; in fact the contrary happens when a house is modified. We say it has "character." We don't like cars with character, with individuality, which is what you get when cars are evolving. We evolve stereo systems by improving components as they are developed, constantly struggling with connectors and compatibility, but at least we get an appropriate machine.

We tend to think of a car as a cell rather than an organ, a

cell that is atomic rather than the symbiotic cluster it really is. For a mobile machine, the car is rather static; it doesn't grow or adapt, except through the generations.

So what we'd like is a car-machine (and transportation in general) that adapts not only in a generational cycle but within its own life cycle. We want a car that is evolving more within the life cycle of us. This makes sense to me because our ideas of what is appropriate and responsible are also changing within our life cycle, and so the evolution of cars must be allowed to keep pace.

How does one engineer a car to be fluid, ever remaking itself? Can you engineer such a thing? I submit that this is Nissan's challenge.

DANICA REMY: Kevin, you are not hanging out with the people who do it. I have been around the classic-car circuit for my entire life, and those people do modify their cars. I, for example, was happy to spend several thousand dollars blueprinting the engine in my 1978 Saab Turbo. In addition, I put sway bars, awesome shocks, hot tires, illegal headlights, and numerous other things to soup it up. Why did I do it? I loved my Saab. I was like the homeowners; rather than spend 25K for a new car, I decided to make my car perform at least as well as the new ones. That was eight years ago. I did go out and buy a used 1987 Saab Turbo four months ago. I will probably trick out the new car also.

PAMELA McCORDUCK: The evolving car as Huber suggests it, and as it is contextualized by Catherine, is the most intriguing idea here so far, in my humble opinion.

KEVIN KELLY: Not knowing how feasible engineering an "evolving" car would be, I called J. Baldwin, trained as a car designer, and *Whole Earth*'s resident eco-tech expert, and

7

1

asked him if it's possible to make cars more customizable, and if so, then why they are not so now. My interpretation of his forty-five-minute answer is:

Cars are midway in complexity between a building (mostly low-tech) and electronics (extremely hi-tech), so that they have the disadvantages of being ruled by harsh physical demands while needing to evolve at a high-tech rate. He felt that litigation and insurance worked against having truly customizable autos. (He tells of insurance reps now being part of car design teams.) Too much liability uncertainty.

He talked about the few failed attempts at partial upgrading of cars. The sheer compact physical complexity (and cost thereof) did them in. The life expectancy of a two-by-four stud is beyond the life expectancy of its owner, but the life expectancy of a wheel bearing may be only ten years. And it's crazy to increase their durability because their design will be revolutionized in ten years. Imagine if you had bought a car that lasted twenty years in 1970, he said. You'd still have it now and it would be getting an awesome 8 miles per gallon. It wouldn't have shoulder harnesses either, or disc brakes, and so on.

Given the huge army of people killed each year in auto accidents, the most responsible improvement we can make toward a responsible car is to make them safer.

J says the general trend in car development is toward big, lighter, safer cars, and niche cars. Since cars are so hard to evolve individually, you compromise by making small numbers of more highly evolved cars. A niche car may be produced in the quantity of 8,000–10,000. He sees three areas of niche cars: the urban runabout, probably electric; the highway cruiser made with boogie-board technology—

foam composites such as airplanes now use; and rental roadrocket minivans, vehicles you rent to haul stuff in or vacation with. Computers are making niche cars possible, in both manufacturing ease and ease of design. You change a chip to change performance of the engine.

The most visible improvements in cars will come about because of law-induced safety concerns. He gave examples of why an evolving car is so difficult to make. Say you want to add an air bag to your existing car. You probably can't. For one thing, your soundproofed, sealed car needs to have special ventilation to ease the tremendous air pressure that occurs in the interior when the air bag is inflated. Without it, it could pierce your eardrums. Two, your steering column probably has sharp things protruding that will puncture the air bag, that is, if it has any room to store it in the first place. The list seemed to go on. It just doesn't add on. Well, it was a nice idea.

ART KLEINER: To some extent, the same add-on issues even apply to computers. Many people tried to upgrade their IBM PCs to the next higher model, the AT clone. Seems like an easy match—but it almost always failed to work correctly with the full complement of software. It'd be like having a car that every now and then balked at driving down certain streets. On the other hand, computers that are specifically designed to anticipate some add-ons, even those that are specifically not anticipated, seem to be okay. Can that be applied to car design?

2

Convenience and Freedom

●

KEES VAN DER HEIJDEN: I once heard a Dow person speak about the "hire-a-chemical" future, based on total recycling of all material streams in society. Nobody would buy any material goods, because everything would be returned after use.

   Could the same happen to cars, i.e., a future where nobody any longer buys his car, or where the purchase price includes a commitment to recycle the current model?

STEWART BRAND: Fascinating idea, Kees.

BARBARA HEINZEN: I like that one, Kees. Hiring the use of something and then returning it.

DOUG CARMICHAEL: What if we had lots of small cars owned by the public car company? They are all white, all clean, and when you find one and want one, you can use it. Leave it legally parked when you arrive, and they are all computer detectable so they appear on your laptop as to location (like the Loran system for small boats), or recoverable just by sight. I remember ten years ago an experiment in Amsterdam with bikes along these lines.

We would need an interesting solution to fuel. Perhaps each user has a credit card and gets billed and also credited when she fills it up. This could also validate licenses and other data necessary for safe driving, and might go with car phones, etc., which could be programmed through the credit-card number. Lots of synergies will make this work.

KEVIN KELLY: Some communes, including the Gaskin Farm in Tennessee, tried the community car and discovered—no surprise—that it didn't work. They found that "everybody's car" was the same as "nobody's car."

GERARD FAIRTLOUGH: What about the vehicle-sharing scheme run by Hertz, Avis, etc? They've got very sophisticated systems for making vehicles available, and they're the people to get into a "Pilot Project for Urban Transport" along with the automakers. Auto companies are happy working with (and sometimes controlling) car-rental companies.

A city would have to be persuaded to cooperate, but if the auto and rental companies were managing and funding the project, that shouldn't be too hard. Apart from buses, trucks, emergency vehicles, etc. (which would require special licenses), all vehicles in the city would have to comply with a strict specification (which for the pilot project would mean that they were produced by the responsible automaker; later, competition could enter).

The specification would ensure that vehicles were highly fuel-efficient (well over 100 miles per U.S. gallon in energy-equivalent terms), light, quiet, and equipped with electronic guidance systems which would deal with gridlock and allow diversions if streets are blocked.

These urban vehicles would be hired at airports, bus and train stations, and interchange points where highways reach the edge of the city (conventional cars could be parked there).

Advantage to the auto and rental firms would be that they could get ahead in vehicle and system design know-how in a field which should expand very rapidly if the pilot project is successful. They would also gain great kudos from success.

PETER GLEICK: It appears that the idea of a long-lasting car that is modified with new components is out of the question (at least in today's environment), but what about the earlier concept of a completely "recyclable" car—not just recyclable, but perhaps required to be recycled?

3

Redefining a Product

●

PETER COYOTE: My two favorite vehicles are, respectively, twenty-five and seventeen years old and both run perfectly. They are easy to repair. They are simple to understand. I like the fact that for seventeen and twenty-five years no one has had to mine iron ore, tap rubber trees, mine copper, chrome, tin, zinc, lead, etc., to build new cars. While my '64 Dodge may not be as clean as some, it is a low-compression engine and does not produces NOx's.

Responsibility should at least include using less of the planet, meaning creating automobiles which are far more durable and simpler to repair (rather than replace). The same should hold true for parts (the old reparable fuel pump vs. the sealed unit, for instance). There is a pleasure in knowing how your tools work and being able to care for them.

Finally, the most responsible car would probably be no car, since it is a luxurious (decadently luxurious) way for individuals to travel, and we really need clean, fast, safe, efficient mass transit. Everyone knows that freight trains are cheaper and more efficient than semi-trucks, but political decisions sidetracked the railroad. Why should we move into the twenty-first century continuing our addiction to cars, unless those cars can integrate with mass transit in some way? (Imagine driving into a station and steering your car onto a track and hooking to the cars fore and aft and being pulled somewhere at 100 mph, and then disengaging and driving two to five miles to another destination.) We can't go on, because certain geographical bottlenecks just slow traffic to the point of madness, and unless we get hydrogen fuel for free, the amount and cost of energy (and pollution) will be staggering. I think consumers are responding to this viscerally with bicycles, where appropriate, driving less, and turning the work of travel into physical fitness.

PAMELA McCORDUCK: "No car" is rather idealized. The world I live in hasn't been designed for such self-denial. If we're talking about tearing up the infrastructure (roads, etc.), let's talk about that. In the foreseeable future, however, that isn't going to happen, so we need to talk about adapting to the infrastructure we have.

We need to talk about the fact that outside the most desirable urban areas folk are being forced to commute four hours (round trip) a day (say, Tracy to Oakland, or central New Jersey to New York or Philadelphia) just because that's where the affordable housing is. How can we undo that with the least pain possible? How can we see that whatever vehicles people use for those excruciating commutes have the least possible impact on the environment?

A car that endures is certainly the first step.

ART KLEINER: Suppose the planners of an auto company decided that the most responsible course they could pursue was what Peter Coyote indirectly suggests: that they should work toward the elimination of the automobile, becoming (thus by necessity) a mass-transit company. Could a company reasonably be expected to seek its own demise (or complete transformation) that way?

Is it the sort of thing that any company, American or Japanese, would want to do? Are we prepared to suggest that it's what auto companies should do?

PETER COYOTE: I am not advocating the dissolution of our infrastructure. The reason people are stuck commuting for so long is because there are cars! Wouldn't it be more "responsible" to the environment if they could drive ten minutes to a train station and take a light rail (perhaps along existing highway rights-of-way)? Isn't the target to turn cars on less, use them less, and need less of them?

Isn't the notion that any individual can drive where and when he wants and marshal the extraction of tons of planetary resources at will a rather decadent one? You are talking to a guy who loves cars—raced them, welded them; tinkers, tunes, repairs, and reads about them—but the facts seem to point toward this target.

The trick is to do it without disrupting society unduly. This might mean fleets of taxis and strict penalties for single driving during commute hours. Obviously, in a democracy everything is negotiable and buyable, but should we not establish the targets? Isn't the most responsible target turning them on less, having less of them, having the ones we have be more durable and less consumptive of natural resources? How we get from here to there will occupy us for some time, I imagine. I think that auto companies should be preemptive about gridlock before the class action suits begin, just as they should be preemptive about safety and the environment. They will be perceived as the source of the problem. Individuals cannot keep up with industry. You cannot recycle cans as fast as a Coke plant can turn them out. The public will perceive their power and capacity for destruction as culpability (even though they participate in it) and the auto manufacturers should lead formulations to solve such problems.

After all, they will be making the light rail systems, or could; they could be designing trains like ferries, which could load your tiny modular car onto trains for the long hauls when you needed your car at the other end. (Imagine going to Los Angeles that way on a bullet train and having your car with you.) Finally, until government policy establishes targets, everything will continue in the same destructive hodgepodge fashion it does today. So what I am arguing out with you (or attempting to) is what the target of policy should be.

PETER SCHWARTZ: The transit-vs.-cars dilemma is a very difficult one. The essential problem is urban density. Transit systems developed naturally in cities where a high level of density was achieved before the car came along, e.g., New York and London. Cars have come to dominate those regions where cars and transit were much more competitive, like the Bay Area. Even allowing for the fact that we had a transit system here and it was dismantled, which might have increased density along the rail line, the broad pattern of urban sprawl has worked against transit and rail in general. The flexibility of the automobile provides a strong motivation to increase sprawl, e.g., the location of shopping, work, and home have many more options in an auto-based system than in a transit-based system.

Even London, with its massive investment in subways and buses, has now hit gridlock. The reason appears to be affluence. As soon as people can afford to, they turn to cars as a means of commuting. Also, there has been a massive growth in short business trips, e.g., an accountant visiting a client. This is the fastest-growing type of trip, and these short trips do not tend to follow the radial pattern of most transit. Such trips more often follow a random grid, making transit very difficult. It is not an accident that, despite subways, the streets of New York are filled with taxis.

PAMELA McCORDUCK: Peter Coyote, we are basically on the same side. I particularly like the idea of targets, as opposed to coercive laws, for all the usual reasons.

I love the idea of car capsules (if I can coin a term for what you describe), piggybacking my personal transportation hither and yon, my personal transportation being small, cozy, safe, well mannered in the social and ecological senses.

Peter, the streets of New York—make no mistake, Manhattan—are filled with taxis (rotten, gutsprung, kidney-stone-jiggling vehicles that they are) because it's still the fastest way to get places! These are not my studies, by the way.

So what I see emerging here is the end of the homogeneous family auto and the beginning, perhaps, of special-purpose transportation modules. One thing to haul the groceries from the supermarket; another thing to get to and from the airport; still another for long but quasi-local trips; still another to piggyback to places where you'll want personal transportation again.

RUSTY SCHWEICKART: Seems Peter Coyote's dockable transporters might offer a more wholistic opportunity. Reserve the inner freeway lanes for high-speed docked units to which individual units could accelerate and dock. Doing so, you would surrender (temporarily) most of your control and signal your willingness to be docked with. When you want out, you undock fore and aft and pull over into the regular lanes, slowing to the "individual" lower speed limit. Let's work on it.

BARBARA HEINZEN: I agree very much with the "ideal" that the best car is *no* car, and that some kind of shift toward greater mass transit is essential, primarily in urban areas. (Rural transport is a very different problem. . . .) I am also willing to agree that the ideal is not easy to achieve and that there are considerable environmental gains to be made by producing simpler and more durable autos and parts.

But I think we can also expand the discussion of responsibility to a consideration of the effect that transport systems have on social organization. Peter Schwartz said that urban sprawl worked against the development of mass transit systems, but, in my view, the causality runs in the other direction: urban sprawl resulted from the lack of mass transit and the encouragement of the "go-anywhere" individualism which is allowed by the automobile and so obviously satisfying to many people.

In turn, it can be argued that urban sprawl has allowed more people to live in larger personal spaces but has also destroyed the social space created by a "downtown." The mall is the epitome of automobile-designed commerce but lacks all the vitality and quirkiness of a centralized street market. It also promotes capital-intensive trading rather than labor-intensive trading and probably expands the gap between haves and have-nots.

Which leads us into a much broader systemic consideration of responsibility and a need to ask: Whose interests do we want to serve first?

PAMELA McCORDUCK: Yes, certainly the construction of the interstate highway system "opened up" places to live that had been difficult at best before those highways came in. In that sense, the roads preceded the sprawl.

Another point: the automobile culture assumes that nobody under age sixteen or past age seventy has any business going anywhere (sixteen being the age to be a licensed driver in California, and seventy being the moment when you start being tested far more carefully). Thus, if the graying of our population here continues, what does that imply for the private auto?

KEES VAN DER HEIJDEN: Car capsules is the proposed mode of operation of the channel tunnel: cars will be put onto trains to make the trip. The interesting thing is that the economic calculations which have been based on people staying in their cars for the trip are now being completely upset by the safety authorities, who consider that totally unacceptable. However, getting people out of their cars into separate carriages is going to be so time-consuming that substantially higher investments are going to be required. Will be interesting to see how this plays out. Construction of the tunnel has not been stopped yet, though.

DOUG CARMICHAEL: If urban areas were linear rather than radial, then public transportation would be fast, along a straight line (or a single curve, like in a natural river valley), and locals and express trains would carry you easily from one part of the long metropolis to another. Access from homes, workplaces, and shops would be easy, if the city is say only four blocks wide. Beyond would be open space, nature, and perhaps bike paths. It is the radial nature of cities that makes the sprawl so hard for transportation. Each intersection requires time for interchange and increases the overhead on maintenance and the possibility of accidents. Curves are hard on equipment.

STEWART BRAND: Doug, I fear you have just restated the theory of suburbs. It failed in important ways ("streetcar" suburbs preceded automobile suburbs). The current theory in "neo-traditional" town planning is based on close-packed street grids; central public spaces and buildings; all amenities walking distance; and plenty of mass transit involving only a maximum of a five-minute walk and a five-minute wait to get a ride. Along rail lines, they're called "pedestrian pockets," which is closer to your scheme.

PETER GLEICK: To paraphrase Amory Lovins, we don't want cars, we want to be able to get from one place to another.

If we, as a society, decide that the continued use of fossil fuels is bad for the environment and bad for the future, then I would argue that it becomes socially responsible for a corporation to begin to shift toward producing non-fossil-fuel-consuming alternatives, and "rethink" itself. The corollary argument, I suggest, is that it is socially irresponsible *not* to begin this shift.

GM and others intend to market an electric car; almost all the manufacturers are playing around with highly efficient gasoline engines; UPS in Los Angeles is shifting to natural-gas-powered vehicles, and so on. Ignoring these first hints of large changes would be irresponsible in the more narrow corporate sense—irresponsible to shareholders, employees, and the company itself. Indeed the penalty for not innovating may be corporate death—the traditional result of failing to adapt to changing conditions, if I may draw a biological/evolutionary parallel. I hope that the next

car I buy will be electric, or at least nongasoline, and recycled (as opposed to recyclable).

DOUG CARMICHAEL: Have we missed a fundamental distinction—between what we use trucks for and what we could
confine cars to? What if all boxes and containers below a
certain size could be distributed on underground conveyor
belts with bar coding? Leave the surface and petrol use to
people? Would that make a major difference in the economics of environmental and cultural impact?

PAMELA McCORDUCK: That's an interesting distinction, Doug.
But really—public transportation ain't so awful when it's
fast and convenient (I say this as a regular New York City
subway rider). As Stewart keeps saying, if you need only
walk five minutes, and then wait five minutes, the "automobile" looks less and less attractive. Trouble is, of course,
most people don't have that five-plus-five alternative.

JACK HUBER: I like the idea brought up by someone else that
we should haul cars on trains. In fact, there is such an
operation between someplace in Virginia and Orlando,
Florida. You drive your car on, hop in a coach, and reverse
the operation at the other end. I heard it was $100 for the
car, plus train fare for the folks.

Within the mega sprawl, I go mass whenever I can. Like
Pamela, I've spent many an hour on the Lex; the RR; the A,
changing at Euclid for the Far Rockaways; the M to Delan-
cey . . . and even the seventh Avenue IRT to the Metro-
politan Opera! I've been on BART; the Metro; Marta up and
down Atlanta, to and from the airport. But I don't have a
whole lot of company. But when I cruise Atlanta's blues
bars, I'm sorry, but mass transit is out of mind and—more
importantly—nowhere near where I want to go.

4

Refining the Product

●

PAMELA McCORDUCK: In a recent New York *Times*, the business column spoke of a simple (hah!) allocation of "commute miles" to all citizens, accumulations to be monitored by onboard automobile computers. If you didn't need your allocation, you could sell your surplus to people who did.

It seemed to me like a scheme to help the rich get richer. That is, my dwellings are conveniently located because I could afford to buy them in convenient locations, because I'm well off. (Worse, my commute to work is into my study, integral to my dwelling.) Thus under such a scheme I could realize even further lucre by selling my surplus commute miles to people whose economic backs are already being broken.

ART KLEINER: If the technology for such a thing exists, it could, however, be used to pay tolls automatically and thus eliminate the traffic jams at most tollbooths (this last, written after an attempt to drive through the Lincoln Tunnel on a Saturday night).

STEVE BARNETT: Is there a contradiction between a corporate sense of responsibility and increasing personal security? If a car company creates a vehicle designed to be very secure in dangerous situations, is that begging off dealing with what created the dangerous situation in the first place?

PAMELA McCORDUCK: I'm not sure I understand the sense of your question. If I buy the equivalent of an armored personnel carrier to convey me hither and yon because I have to deal with rogue truckers, should both my car company and I be hammering on the trucking firms? Navistar? Is that what you're asking?

BARBARA HEINZEN: Surely, Steve, your question relates to the issue of controllable space. A car company can sell a safer car but has no authority (or ability?) to alter the system which created the dangerous conditions in the first place.

Which perhaps leads us into the question of how individual responsibility relates to systemic change—the first being immediate and tangible; the second being remote and intangible. What are the mechanisms for linking individual and systemic responsibility?

KEES VAN DER HEIJDEN: Steve, making the car safer all the time is exercising your responsibility in too small a box. For example, in a larger frame, you are dealing with risk-compensation behavior by the motorist, which needs to be factored in.

STEVE BARNETT: Barbara and Kees, what if five car companies presented a collective proposal for developing a "smart" highway system that monitored space between vehicles to the United States Government as their best shot at improving safety vs. building more tanklike individual vehicles? This doesn't immediately strike me as absurd.

BARBARA HEINZEN: Steve's proposal that five car companies

get together to design a highway system may be the start of something new. Particularly if it includes the interplay of mass and individual transit systems.

PETER WARSHALL: Volvo has started a new department to analyze and plan for new cities. They probably hope to design a city with their new vehicle. Nevertheless, they have not waited for five car companies to get together. Göteborg already has limited downtown access for private autos. But Volvo tends to have a long cultural history of conscience, guilt, humanity, and design expertise.

5

You May Start With Bells and Whistles, but You End Up With a Revolution

●

KEES VAN DER HEIJDEN: Here is the challenge:

How can we design a 75-mpg, lightweight car that would give its occupants a chance against the big vehicles on the road? What about the inflatable bags that Iacocca was bragging about the other day?

PETER COYOTE: I am living in Vancouver, and have been without a car for two months. I can walk everywhere for shopping, cleaners, VCRs, recreation, etc. My family came to visit, and I rented a car for a short trip which now sits idle since they left. I prefer not driving when I can.

Do we really want a jillion lightweight 75-mpg cars? That just saves gas! What about all the host of other ills that individual cars engender? Or what about making your little 75-mpg clipper modular so that it could clip onto a train or moving highway lane or something? It seems to me that "personal transportation" is the larger consideration and "car" is a specific subset, one possible solution to the problem. Perhaps "car companies" should begin to consider themselves as "transportation companies" and address the whole spectrum of subsets from mass to singular transportation.

Also, what about the figures on the net energy cost of individual cars? I read a study years ago which showed that trains are the hands-down winners at efficiency in hauling freight. Well, is the car the hands-down winner? Because somewhere along the line we are going to be dealing with the real costs (largest sense of the word) of energy and we could start now.

BARBARA HEINZEN: Back to the point that the "responsible" car is *no* car. What then is the organization, political and spatial, of a postautomobile society?

PAMELA McCORDUCK: I think a no-car society will not be feasible in the next two decades. But I may be wrong. I got to thinking about the enormous need to fix up the highways and bridges which we are all aware of, especially in the eastern U.S. (though the West has its problems too), and wonder if, instead of fixing up the bad old roads and bridges, this might not be an opportunity to rethink the whole design?

STEWART BRAND: The number that one hears is 500,000 U.S. bridges in need of repair. It won't take too many of them falling to make cars useless, "responsible" or not.

PETER SCHWARTZ: It is very clear that people in most societies around the world take nearly every opportunity to increase their freedom of mobility within the car as the "freest" . . . somehow a sense of responsibility must be compatible with that exercise of freedom, because people seem to take it.

BARBARA HEINZEN: I confess that the "postauto" society I had in mind is not necessarily one where cars do not exist. Instead, I was thinking of the progression from horse and foot locomotion to trains to automobiles, and wondering what is the organization of the future.

At the moment, personal motorized transport is dominant. What will be dominant twenty years from now? What mixture of means, organized along what kinds of geographical lines? I see a return to more concentrated forms, so that suburban sprawl begins to collect around transportation nodules of some kind, for example.

STEVE BARNETT: It may be too easy to say the "responsible" car is, hey presto, no car at all. What about the more mundane, perhaps more realistic, task of trying to get agreement among us on what an actual responsible car would look like? What raw materials, how processed, what kind of manufacturing techniques, what would the "responsible" car actually be (features, inside and out), how would it be used, recycled, discarded, etc.? We also need some realism here, like admitting the fun of driving an RX-7. Do we really want a no-frills econobox, or do we cherish our rolling stereo, air conditioning, quiet drive, etc.?

PAMELA McCORDUCK: Thanks, Steve. I was beginning to feel like I'd got into a struggle session instead of a conference when I had the temerity to admit I enjoy my toy. Tell me I'm wrecking the ozone layer, tell me I'm speeding women into widowhood and children into orphanhood, and I'd give it up, but on the list of adult idiocies, it didn't seem so awful. (And anyway, in four years I haven't yet put 20,000 miles on it, so it's really a toy.)

We've been concentrating on the internal combustion

9
1

engine and its discontents. This may be the worst single feature of our present cars. Can anybody give me an ordered list of next worst features?

KEES VAN DER HEIJDEN: Like Peter, I just cannot see people giving up their hard-won personal mobility. Next point: I see global warming as the dominant threat resulting from the use of cars, dwarfing almost any other. The world may not see that yet, but it is only a matter of time before that message will be driven home hard. That's why I come to the following first priorities:

· reduce the economic need for moving around;
· increase fuel efficiency.

The first point is not within the power of the car company to bring about, but the second surely is.

BARBARA HEINZEN: I am not suggesting that we give up cars completely, but surely we must give up some use of cars for some functions. What I am trying to ask is: What are the functions the car now performs which can be performed more "responsibly" in some other way?

PETER GLEICK: Pamela, you're (and I'm) destroying the ozone layer (and contributing to the greenhouse effect).

Kees, I agree entirely that the issue of global climatic change may lead to the first real reexamination of the automobile on "global" environmental grounds.

THE

CORPORATION

1

Mapping the Corporate Ecosystem

●

GERARD FAIRTLOUGH: I'd like to describe a model of capitalism which may help us to understand the limits on corporate responsibility and how to push out those limits.

Think of information as either codified or uncodified. Codified information is simple, precise, compressing complexity into specific descriptions or quality. Example: food quality, stock market quotations, demographic data. Uncodified information is rich, often uncertain, often tacit, sometimes poetic.

My model pictures the business firm as a compartment within which uncodified information is freely used for communication. This is because the people involved have a shared language and a shared stock of concepts, which allow them to cope with complexity and imprecision. Outside the boundary of the company, codified information, with its comprehensibility and simplicity, is the main medium of communication. This is a simplistic model, but probably not more so than the famous model of the Invisible Hand, which has lasted for two hundred and fourteen years.

What does this say about corporate responsibility? Corporations can respond easily to codified requirements—defined safety or environmental standards, easily measured consumer preferences, moral standards as simple as some of the Ten Commandments. But giving the corporation an ecological web and expecting them to follow its ramifications will be asking for superficial or erratic responses, whatever the integrity or personal beliefs of the individuals in the corporation.

Corporations can be proactive in codification, e.g., Steve Barnett's idea of five car companies devising a proposal for safe highway systems or for solutions to gridlock (see "Refining the Product," p. 86). But don't expect corporations to cope with lots of uncodified information. However sincere a corporation is about making its internal workings transparent, the fact that these workings depend on uncodified information will make it hard for the public really to understand what is going on.

Based on these ideas about the nature of capitalism, here is a proposal for an initiative which could be taken by a "responsible" corporation.

STEP 1 CHOOSING PRIORITIES: The corporation chooses around seven priorities for responsible action. These should be varied and imaginative and designed to catalyze much wider action by other corporations, by governments, and by other bodies. They could range from pilot schemes to worldwide targets.

The process of selection of the priorities is most important. There should be widespread debate, inside and outside the corporation, and should start with a long list of possible priorities from which the seven or so are chosen. The whole process should be as transparent as possible. All the priorities should have well-defined targets against which progress can be measured reasonably objectively. Achievement of the target could take up to ten years, but intermediate targets should be set for every two to three years.

STEP 2 REPORTING PROGRESS: For each priority, a panel of outside observers is set up. These should include experts, eminent people, and ordinary folk. They would have the right to investigate progress toward the target, resources to do this, and ways to report their findings widely. Mutual trust between the corporation and the panel would be needed without compromising the panel's independence.

STEP 3 CHANGING PRIORITIES: Priorities can be changed. When targets have been met, it may be right to shift attention to another field. It may turn out that some of the originally chosen priorities were wrong. And new areas of importance may emerge. A process for changing priorities is therefore needed, but it should be as transparent and consultative as the process for the original choice of priorities, and it would be a serious failure if most of the original priorities did not continue for five years or more.

STEP 4 INFLUENCING OTHERS: The responsible corporation wants to be seen as responsible and to benefit thereby. It also wants to influence world conditions. An effective communication program is needed to tell the world about the process of priority choice, what the priorities chosen are, what are the targets set, and about progress in actioning them. A vigorous effort to influence others to adopt similar processes and priorities is also needed. This may persuade governments to set industry standards or persuade other corporations to follow. The aim should be both to

9
7

achieve business advantage for the responsible corporation and to effect lasting improvement in society.

I'd like to hear whether any of you think this makes some sense. If it does, we could explore some specific examples of priorities which a Japanese-based, multinational automobile manufacturer could adopt, and how consultation, transparency, and monitoring could be achieved across the world.

DOUG CARMICHAEL: On first reading I like it. The idea of looking at "responsibility" as an information-flow problem, and of modeling it explicitly as such, seems to give a potential handle on the problem that makes players do what they have to, given the information (financial, and all others), and thus reduces our tendency to look at it moralistically and find some players who are doing it wrong.

There is a deeper clue in the origin of "responsibility": "spond" comes from giving allegiance or faith to another, and "re-spond" has its earliest meanings in a use like responsive readings in church, where the text is known but uttered by the multitude. This means that responsibility is really a highly constrained process. That's why looking at the whole as information flow might get us out of a jam of moralism.

STEWART BRAND: I greatly like the distinction between codified and uncodified information outside and within the organization "boundary." Gregory Bateson used to complain that about all that was translated accurately between cultures was numbers, and this led to impoverished and destructive dialogue.

KEES VAN DER HEIJDEN: Gerard, your point on uncodified knowledge is right on. It is recognized (more in Japan than in the West) as one of the invisible assets (see Itami's well-known book). At a deep level it is the source of all competitive advantage, because it is not emulatable.

I suppose you are suggesting that a company also has uncodified knowledge about its responsibility. Your proposal would be a process to surface it to the codified level, in order that it can become the source of external action. Is this the purpose of the external "responsibility" board?

I rather like your ideas because they would be a way out of the dilemmas we have surfaced in this conference between "responsibility" and survival. I think you may have suggested a synergetic way out by putting the discussion at a higher level. If I understand you right, the practical conclusion is that, before deciding on what constitutes today's "responsible" car, Nissan should "mine" its rich internal uncodified knowledge as it pertains to responsibility, and engage in a process to make it actionable, e.g., by means of an external "responsibility" board.

Maybe this conference could play such a role. (A new use for computerized conferencing?)

CATHERINE BATESON: Are there certain messages which people only accept in codified form? I agree with the strength of the uncodified, but we should ask the mirror question.

One clue: many people who do not individually make "responsible" choices will vote for legislation that will enforce responsibility.

PETER WARSHALL: Gerard, I did not understand if you felt that the ecological web was codified or uncodified. Or if some people (ecologists) know the codes but others (car corporations) do not. Is the job of ecologists to teach the corporations how to codify the ecological web into the corporate process? Or did I miss something here?

We also run into the problem not of codified vs.

noncodified but of which code. The Bush administration has chosen a global-warming model (codified knowledge) that differs from those of some meteorologists. In some circumstances, it's a matter of how to switch codes.

Kees believes that your further abstraction helps clarify. I am not quite sure.

P.S. If you want to talk of the codification of the eco-web, we can. Even as it pertains to cars.

To follow up one step further, I would promote the idea of all corporations setting ten-year priorities and monitoring them. What I think is new is the incorporation of ecologists and even environmentalists (i.e., ecologists with political goals) into the formulation of priorities.

SAS had me review their holding companies to see if they were "green" enough to advertise it. This was my first attempt at such an evaluation. I think I discouraged SAS because I did not explain that no corporation or human is green enough to meet contradictory forces active on the planet. It would have been better to set up your process and have SAS advertise as the first corporation to use the process. The priorities would have included European Greens.

I would emphasize my belief, following Catherine, that people respond in "contradictory" ways, with uncodified info dictating choices as much as codified. To add to all this, consider low riders, probably the most elegant poor man's car rehab in the U.S. Incredible artists are actually showing up in San Jose and Tucson with long discussions of candy-layered paint (up to seven) and the Hispanic romantic figurine traditions (women standing on roaring black panthers, etc.).

Personally, I have an Isuzu Trooper and care little for vehicles except to get me somewhere to walk or explore. I know a Toyota Land Cruiser is better but can't afford one. The Isuzu is typical of the great surge in the U.S. of small trucks and Jeep Cherokee "switch hitter" vehicles. Jeeps, for instance, are a metalanguage for the out-of-doors. They are terrible difficult-road or off-road vehicles. They carry a "wild" image for suburban use. Land Rovers are topheavy (I flipped in one). I chose the Isuzu for a combination of increased comfort over my old Ford pickup and because so many friends wanted to go to Mexico with me. Like Danica (see "The Evolve-It-Yourself Product," p. 67), I will modify it for sleeping, and add gasoline tanks, water carriage, botanical built-in worktable, etc., as money allows. I mean, I like fiddling with my vehicle as Danica does—she with classics, me for the ultimate "safari" vehicle.

I would like to add that humans always decide how laws apply to them. Every human who drinks will decide not just what the law says but what he/she feels capable of handling. Laws are general. People have different capacities. The same applies to speed limits and the road conditions, and seat belts and the traffic. I never wear a seat belt in the outback. They are for head-on collisions. When my Land Rover flipped, the woman in the seat belt hurt her body more than I did because the seat belt limits movability. In other words, codes exist in contexts. Societies make rules that are somewhat noncontextual. Citizens "tailor" the codes to internal beliefs and external realities. Perhaps there is a future in the "niche car."

Finally, we should distinguish whom we are representing when we talk; I find this confusing. As a powerful corporate elite trying to shape the future, many of the GBN* mem-

* Global Business Network of Emeryville, California, is an international think tank and consulting firm that was instrumental in organizing this electronic conference.

bers speak on the multinational level. Then they speak as individuals or for their families. We are not "wholes" or even wholistic in these voices. But responsibility comes, in part, from becoming aware of the number of different voices in which we speak and consciously working with them.

GERARD FAIRTLOUGH: Let's assume that a Japanese-based automobile manufacturer has set up a framework for choosing priorities, setting targets within the priority areas, and monitoring progress. Here are some possible priorities within a framework of that kind:

1. PILOT PROJECT FOR URBAN TRANSPORT (see "Convenience and Freedom," pp. 74–76)

2. VEHICLE SAFETY STANDARDS

Automakers are rightly held strictly responsible for accidents caused by malfunction of their products, and also have much responsibility for protecting users of their products from the effects of accidents, however caused. But what if they assumed responsibility for any accident in which, at first sight, the product was not a cause (e.g., if it were hit by another vehicle while it was stationary)?

Cars have an influence on their drivers and on others. They should be easily seen by others but should not provoke emotions which could lead to accidents. Advertising of cars could lead their drivers or others into dangerous behavior. If automakers are committed to the reduction of accidents, they might start supporting changes in highway design; urban traffic systems installation; legal codes; driver education; and so on, at least as far as these things affect the safety of their products.

Adopting a standard such as a halving of accidents per person-mile in which the "responsible" corporations' products were in any way involved would be a risky move. But if the standards were met, the advantage to the automaker could be great: image, lower insurance premiums, government support.

3. VEHICLE EMISSIONS

If a large responsible auto corporation committed itself to a decade of improving exhaust standards, this should force others to follow. The advantage to the "responsible" corporation would be that the schedule for improvements would be its own, rather than one imposed on it by others.

4. VIEWS OF JAPAN IN THE WEST

Suspicions about Japan pervade Western countries. All Japanese-based multinational corporations must be concerned that these suspicions will cause them problems and must wish to reduce them. But what can a single firm (even a big one) do? I suggest that a target for improving matters in one particular area would be realistic, especially if it were part of a sustained ten-year program making use of all communications such as advertising and point-of-sale publicity. Measurement of progress in an area like this wouldn't be easy. Public-attitude surveys are the obvious first approach; changes in the way the media report things is another.

As a suggestion for a particular theme which a "responsible" automaker could adopt: what about *Design?* Would a greater public appreciation of the Japanese contribution to culture and practical affairs throughout the world, by excellence and flair in design, help to change attitudes to Japan in general? Would knowledge of Japan's contribution to gardens, calligraphy, painting, and ceramics lead to an appreciation that a design tradition of this kind helps enormously to produce today's attractive clothes and consumer products (including cars) and helps to create an admirably civilized society? And good design is about economy. As in brush strokes, so in use of natural resources.

Catherine Bateson's plea (see "The Evolve-It-Yourself Product," pp. 68–69) that we give a sense of the biological to our transactions with the environment is just right. As well as artifacts that evolve, we need organizations and systems of governance which evolve. As Ian Mitroff [Topic 1 page 117] says, all institutions must continually redesign themselves. But there are limits on what institutions can do, since they are subject to constraints—political, financial, and credibility—by the people they must attract into the institution. Institutions behave like members of a shoal of sticklebacks, mainly moving together, although some of the fish are more independent than others. We should hope to influence both the shoal and the individual fishes. Push the adventurous individuals up to, but not beyond, the point when they rush back to join the shoal.

My sense of how fish behave in Japan is that being in the

shoal is very important, but the shoal as a whole is more adventurous than in the West.

JIM PELKEY: Building on the use of ecological web: the responsible corporation would work with other corporations in its industry to establish "responsibility" goals that would be common to the industry, even potentially allowing joint R&D in order to maximize the chances of success.

It seems to me that the responsible corporation is at significant economic risk if it behaves responsibly at the same time that its competitors act with short-term goals such as lower prices, reduced R&D expenditures, lower service levels. The offending corporation could get away with this behavior for maybe a few years, just long enough to give the "responsible" corporation fits.

Again the issue of government is begged. Who is (are) the right third party(s) to review and validate broad, long-term goals?

GERARD FAIRTLOUGH: I'm glad some of you like the codified/uncodified information distinction. More about it in these papers:

Max Boisot and John Child, "The Iron Law of Fiefs," *Admin. Science Quarterly*, 33 (1988), 507ff.
Gerard Fairtlough, "A Model of Capitalism Derived From Communication Theory, *Futures*, Jan./Feb. 1990, 39ff.

Gregory Bateson's complaint about impoverished development (see Stewart Brand's comment on p. 98) ties in with Jurgen Habermas's vision of systems based on codified information: "Colonizing the Lifeworld."

Kees, yes, my suggestion relates to the "mining" of uncodified information, but externally as well as internally, and in relation to corporate action generally, not only "responsible" cars. Incidentally, I had in mind an external responsibility board for each major responsibility area.

Catherine, yes, codified information has great power and sometimes dreadful results like reducing people to stereotypes or objects.

Peter Warshall, the idea I have of a web is something of great complexity and, hence, uncodified. But not all webs are like that and, if ecologists can reduce complexity into a codified web which can become part of the corporate or governmental thinking, that would be very useful (also potentially dangerous—ref. the Bush administration/global warming example).

My point is that corporations are probably incapable of being responsible unless the area of responsibility is well defined and unless perceptions about what it means to be "responsible" are widely shared.

CATHERINE BATESON: A few more words on codified vs. uncodified. First, I would say that understanding and describing a system need not make it a codified system. In particular, the description of an ecological web does not make it a codified system, because I take the word "codified" to exist in the context of "codified vs. uncodified," with different attitudes attached and different orders of flexibility, and it is that contrast which is absent in ecology. Furthermore, I can describe with some precision the rules whereby two Iranians decide who shall pay a restaurant check or walk first through a door, and most Iranians can also express this with only a tiny bit of Socratic help. But I don't think that makes it a "codified" system. And when it is violated, no one can turn around and say, "You didn't follow the rules." Something like this is central to the human contrast between

codified and uncodified. The person who violates uncodified systems is regarded with dislike, unease, maybe as a
bounder or a cad . . . but is not, so to speak, indictable.

Now notice that I used two English slang words above,
"bounder" and "cad." That is because I suspect the uncodified English system has more resilience than the U.S. at
present. But scenarios for the future: at present in this country we seem to believe that codification is the road to uto-
pia—most noticeable in the ambition to legislate ethics at
every level. Now why does a society go that route? Because
when you have a lot of rapid change and a lot of cultural
diversity the old uncodified consensus isn't there any more.
People can't function by rules that are *sous-entendu*, and indeed, even though I know and follow this or that traditional
convention, I increasingly resent the fact that others get
away with breaking it, so I want to make a law. Unfortunately, human society needs a substantial dose of ambigu-
ity, and trying to specify everything is a *reductio ad absurdum*
(partly because you have to specify the specification process, and so on, recursively).

Some of this, of course, has always been true of the U.S.
because of the kind of society it is (immigration); but I
think a lot of people came out of the sixties determined to
change the world by codification—that is, not really
changing from within any more. Companies and institutions can maintain elegant internal cultures, or indeed multiple internal cultures in different divisions.

The critical question is whether conventions and attitudes change in healthy ways around attempts at codification. If so, then, e.g., affirmative-action hiring procedures
help. If not, they may hinder, but depicting black folk in
senior positions on TV may help, etc. The point I made

earlier was that I will happily comply with a recycling law or a miles-per-gallon law or pay higher taxes for transport or housing or social programs, but when I express a personal commitment to these things, without laws I may feel ripped off, and indeed I become very selective.

PETER COYOTE: My supposition is that corporations will do no more or less than they must. The problem is that they treat one class of citizen (the stockholders) as favored and skew their policies toward those interests. This effectively divides and fragments community and makes one quadrant "pay" somehow, some way, for the other quadrant's trip. I have the suspicion that this may be a limit of business and that we need another model to address issues which affect all social quadrants simultaneously.

PETER SCHWARTZ: For me, the concept of responsibility has to do with a sense of obligation (encompassing both liability and a positive, creative need to make things better). I often feel that, in some companies, the social milieu is a sense of mutual obligation, while in others there is a sense of mutual victimization. I have no obligation to someone who is victimizing me.

JOHN ROZSA: My response to the notion of the responsible corporation, consumer, and product was to think in broader terms. Consumers, corporations, and products are involved in a complex interactive system. Consumers not only buy products produced by corporations, they work directly for corporations or they provide services that people who work for corporations pay for. Yet corporations are governed by the so-called hard realities of the market, driven by business cycles and the need to stay competitive. As such, they have no loyalties to people who might not be overcome by economics.

Thus it is hard for me to take seriously the idea of "responsible products" being more than a superficial ploy that
would appeal only to credulous consumers. For if corporations have no fundamental loyalties to people, how can we
believe they might be responsible to the more abstract notion of the environment?

PETER WARSHALL: We must step back and help corporations
and consumers define their "circle of responsibility." With
cars, the steps go like this:

A. Harvesting or mining raw materials
B. Processing the raw materials into usable parts
C. Assembling the parts (manufacture)
D. Using the product
E. Discarding the product
F. Recycling or reusing discarded parts or materials
G. Transport between each of these steps

I will give some senses of responsibility. Cars are made of
aluminium (in part) that is strip-mined in Jamaica, Guyana,
and Zimbabwe. Are producers or consumers responsible for
the devastation caused by these uncontrolled mining operations (or, for that matter, the health conditions of the
workers)? Cars use petroleum products for both gasoline
and plastics. How much responsibility do they have for oil
spills since their products create the demand? How much
responsibility do car companies have for the overflowing
solid waste dumps that cannot recycle the new plastics?
What are the true advantages of aluminum since it requires
such huge amounts of energy to process compared to iron?
These are just the beginnings of looking at corporate
responsibility that has been forced mostly to concentrate
on health and safety issues. Do human health and safety

issues take precedence over residuals (e.g., pollutants in the process that cause fish kills)?

As a starter, I would say there are no values that are not embedded in the ecology of the corporation. The first step is to simply inform: what do we know about the corporation's ecological web? From this, the magnitude of the many problems can be assessed. Perhaps the new compassion for Earth and humans will come from the addition of "quantity" to ethics. I already see in this dialogue some participants wanting or yearning for simple nonquantified ethics—this is good, this is bad. We will always do something to hurt the Earth in order to survive. That's why sophisticated pagans had prayers. But more provincial postmodern urbanites are not curious about the seventeen elements of the Earth that allow them to drive to work. (Just to get the "religious" angle going here!)

If we agree to embedded values and hard-nosed ecological analysis, then we can proceed to the economic concerns like discounting and internal rates of return.

PAMELA McCORDUCK: Three different views of the corporation:

The first talks about its responsibilities being only to profits and self-aggrandizement.

The second presents an ordered list of how the corporation has moved, first from responsibility only to owners, then to stockholders, then . . .

Warshall talks about a corporate ecological web. I'd appreciate further clarification.

ART KLEINER: To what extent does membership in a web (for corporation or individual) imply responsibility for the web?

BARBARA HEINZEN: Good question. I like the notion of an

ecological web, and consider that a corporation has responsibility for both the "upstream" and "downstream" lines of that web. But responsibility without authority is not worth much, and the further away from the corporation that decisions are made, the less viable is the corporation's exercise of any theoretical responsibility.

KEVIN KELLY: Responsibility is always to something or someone. It's a form of relationship and communication. It seems the reason that this conference exists is because who/what corporations are responsible to is shifting. A short history:

Company is responsible to (1) owners; (2) the product or service (guarantee, etc.); (3) the customer, beyond the product (liability); (4) society, beyond the customer (social liability); (5) infrastructure (environment, Earth, etc.); (6) the future.

The reality is a number of businesses are moving from responsibility to the customer to responsibility to society. Few institutions of any stripe are actively responsible to the future because of the countervailing forces against long-term planning. One may have a real responsibility to the environment without necessarily being responsible to the future. For instance, one could have a lumber company that stopped clear-cutting but did not develop new techniques, species, or new kinds of lumber for future use.

DON MICHAEL: Kevin, can you reconcile your "The reality is that businesses are moving from [responsibility to the customer to responsibility to society]" (topic 1, above) with Peter Warshall's description of Clean Air Bill lobbying?

"Just back from Washington D.C. where they are comparing the 750-page-long House and Senate versions of the

Clean Air Bill. To give you an idea of what happens (names changed to protect profits), listen:

"An Abu Dhabi multinational wants to finish construction of the world's largest methanol plant so hires a lobbyist to change by parts per million the requirements for benzene which are different between the congressional bills. Tens of millions of dollars rest on these numbers. Other lobbyists see that ethanol will only enter the industry with an "agricultural subsidy" so they work for keeping the subsidies while the natural gas lobbyists (predominantly methanol and including various AmerIndian tribes) push for no subsidies. Meanwhile, the oil companies (with a single lobbying firm) are pushing for reformulated gasoline in order to maintain market control. California is the leader in all this and so Rusty's CEC is lobbied like crazy because the news, as usual in cars, will be made in California.

"Meanwhile, in Europe, there is a movement against catalytic converters, which use strategic metals such as platinum. In the U.S., out-of-date environmentalists have joined with the catalytic-converter lobby in the name (everybody cheer) of clean air. But other embryonic groups of enviros (everything with an *o* is shortened in D.C.; "ignoramuses" become "ignos") see the light and realize that "preventive" cures such as better fuels will compensate for "postignition treatment." Yes, politics is a muddle and economics and ecology are truly entangled with greed, idealism, and love-of-the-fight having as much energy as usual."

As I read him, I'd say, if the word "responsibility" applies at all, it is to the owner.

Kees writes: "Why should we feel any responsibility to anyone except ourselves?" and then explains how come, pointing out that, while there is a societal consensus, it is "not clear at all . . . what society expects from us" (see "What Should Responsibility Cost—and Who Should Pay?" p. 119).

Is there any longer such a consensus? Was there ever? If there is, will it last? My answer to each is "No." But boundaries established local consensuses (e.g., honor among thieves). Now the boundaries are disappearing or are already gone.

STEWART BRAND: Building (or violating) Warshall's interest in the internal and external corporate ecological web, there is James Lovelock's recent addition to Darwinian theory—a species which actively harms or passively fails to mend its environment will not long prosper. An example of a good organism in this light: trees. A bad organism: cattle.

In Don's border [boundary] terms, where does "environment" begin and end?

When I first heard the term "business environment" at Royal Dutch/Shell I remember smiling wide, thinking, "Gooood terminology, leading in the right direction."

CATHERINE BATESON: First a story. Several years ago I was approached by a researcher attempting to apply some standard instruments (translated) in Iran, studying employee satisfaction. One of the things that tripped him up was that his subjects were totally negative about "responsible" jobs. Americans want "responsible" jobs, a mix of autonomy and efficacy. The standard translation for "responsible" in Farsi actually means something between accountable and answerable—more precisely, that you can get into trouble. We have to look at this double-sidedness: under what circumstances are we talking about interference and guilt, un-

1
1
3

der what circumstances are we inviting corporations, etc., to accept real leadership? Can we format "responsible" so that it is desirable rather than just one more burden?

The efficacy side is very important. Ethical questions only arise where there are choices, and thus it is expectable that every new technology will present new dilemmas (cf. in-vitro fertilization). One thing that seems very important for corporations to do is to offer choices to consumers, not to force them to buy "responsible" cars, but at least to give them a chance. (I once, in a polite tone but, I thought, extraordinarily rudely, asked a manufacturer of junk food for Third World countries if his company made anything that was nutritious and he answered cheerfully that they were just starting a new line. Well, bravo, actually.)

If we can describe a responsible car, then, surely, Step 1 is to make it an available model.

Efficacy—its relationship with power. Lord Acton's, "All power tends to corrupt," etc. Someone once said to me, "All responsibility ennobles." But often, in a given situation, one individual perceives responsibility and another in the same situation perceives power. When you realize you can act, then perhaps you accept responsibility. But some people neglect their children, while others gratify a wish for power by abusing them.

PETER WARSHALL: The ecological web: all labor and industry (even financial industry) is connected to natural resources: minerals, soil, water, plants, animal life, energy, air. The ecological web is simply an accounting of the corporation in these seven ways. It has no internal values. It is thinking eco scenarios. It can simply reveal, perhaps, new ways that a corporation can increase efficiencies and reduce depletion and harm to natural resources. Again, I would say, try it for

your industry: be it movies, garden tools, petroleum, fi-
nances. We could discuss the difficulties on line. I think
this contextual exercise would be more useful than too general (nonecological) attempts to discover responsibility.

After this first step, the questions about how you evaluate
harms (both financial and other) can be made from the eco
flowchart. This sounds very formal but I'm trying to be
practical. It's like doing a family tree when an anthropologist first enters a "foreign" society to discover kin terms.

JIM PELKEY: I am struck with the pessimistic and negative
attitude toward corporations. An attitude that I disagree
with, not that there isn't behavior that I find objectionable
or shortsighted. People have to organize themselves to ac-
complish the complexity of tasks required of a growing
population, be they either health, survival, entertainment,
etc. Competition has also proven to be a very effective
means to bring out the best and to respond to the needs of
consumers.

Corporations have another key responsibility (should be
No. 2 in Kevin's list), that toward employees.

Fundamentally, no corporation can be responsible in any
sense of the word if it does not exist and thrive. The corporation cannot be an active agent of change if it does not
exist or does not have the resources to act. Also, while
corporations may be fictitious to some, I can assure you
that corporations are real and stimulate strong emotions,
commitment, and sense of identity. The evil is not the
corporation—unless, of course, one does not share the
opinion that the free marketplace has demonstrated a
unique ability to provide needed goods and services to individual consumers with individual tastes—but rather the
lack of dimensionality in measuring and rewarding success.

The free market works—it may, however, be trying to op-
timize or maximize too limited an objective function, i.e.,
profits.

But that is where governments come in. They can change
the name of the game; witness the California utility industry. Therefore, can new marketplace goals that better reflect the long-term *full* costs of today's actions be imple-
mented? I believe that car companies have been responding
to the economic goal of a car for every adult, hence low
cost and wide availability and flexibility of choice. When
prices of gas went up, the Japanese gained advantage because they had been designing for a high-cost-of-energy
market. Higher energy price is clearly a step toward full
costing.

Lastly, while we who have the freedom of choice can
debate, there are many who have little and want more.
Since it is impractical to take from those who have, the
drive to create more is fundamental. Therefore, what is our
responsibility to those who do not have or to those who
come after us? It is clear that a healthy environment is one
responsibility that has to be passed on in a stable social
world which is characterized by freedom of choice. But
how to create overarching goals and reward systems that
balance the short-term materialistic needs with the long-
term environmental or quality-of-life requirements? How
do we cause the political system to be farsighted when the
reelection process is every few years?

KEES VAN DER HEIJDEN: Ecological web accounting. Come to
think about it, is ecological web accounting not a variation
of the old input-output table? If everybody were doing this
for himself, we would have to get into each other's operation in some detail, and there would be an awful lot of

duplication of work. I wonder whether it would not be sensible to do it all at once, centrally, the way we produce input-output tables.

JACK HUBER: Don started us off with the suggestion that three parties are participants in this issue: consumers, automobiles, and manufacturers. I suggest we include a fourth in which the other three operate—the community.

We seem to have been talking about the community without using the word. Most of the emphasis on responsibility in this topic has dealt with the environment: discussions of cleanup; moves from cars to mass/public transit; responsibility for various kinds of pollution, etc. As an aside, it does seem ironic that a group of individualistic people (we) are suggesting a move from individual transport (freedom?) to a common, homogeneous one.

IAN MITROFF:

1. The dictionary informs us that the word "responsibility" is a derivative of "respond." One of "respond's" root meanings is "to promise." Two of the primary meanings of "responsible" are (a) "to be answerable to" and (b) "to be accountable to."

2. Over the course of this century, all institutions have continually broadened their reach and influence such that they affect a continually growing number of stakeholders.

3. As a result, *all* institutions have the minimum responsibility to:

    a) Instigate a serious program of crisis management to lessen threats to the environment; e.g., *Exxon Valdez*, one of the most obscene acts;

    b) Plan seriously for *future generations*;

    c) Continually *redesign themselves* and *their products* to accomplish (a) and (b) above;

d) Recognize that all institutions are *systemic* and must be designed and managed as such, e.g., include Americans on the boards and *top management* of Japanese companies. *And vice versa.*

4. The auto companies are no longer in the transportation biz but equally in the entertainment or "UnReality Biz," education, and city planning businesses, to mention only a few.

5. Without the recognition of these points, the responsibility question is virtually meaningless.

PETER GLEICK: The question of differing notions of "responsibility" must acknowledge that there are inherent contradictions between what might be responsible to the general society and what might be responsible to shareholders of a corporation.

For example, wouldn't you consider it responsible to society for the auto companies to not only support but push for higher automobile efficiency standards? But, in reality, they almost uniformly oppose them, because they consider their responsibility to be to the company (and some perceived set of values) and not to the broader society.

Unless this dilemma, these contradictions, are addressed, the idea of corporate responsibility will remain muddled and, worse, ineffective at changing policies and actions.

2

What Should Responsibility Cost—and Who Should Pay?

●

KEES VAN DER HEIJDEN: The meaning of the word "responsibility" has really changed rather fundamentally over the last few decades. In the past responsibility derived from higher authorities; now we are more on our own. Why should we feel any responsibility to anyone except ourselves?

I think that, today, responsibility is something like an attractor state in a highly nonlinear system. It has something to do with a broad societal consensus on how people need to behave toward each other in general, without a confusing reference to any specific instance. This is a very low-frequency phenomenon; any change in this consensus tends to be slow drift, with the exceptional watershed, when the system goes for a hierarchical restructuring.

The consensus is low frequency, but not our individual attitude to each aspect of it. Our own interest fluctuates violently; we cannot always agree with what the consensus tells us, particularly when it conflicts directly with our self-interest in a specific case. In those circumstances, we would like to redefine our responsibility. However, these episodes tend to be short-lived compared to the broad thrust of the societal consensus, and in most cases intensive mutual inter-action with the rest of society, which we cannot avoid, will ensure that we will be pulled back to the attractor and "mend our ways." I do not think we define our own respon-sibility. The culture imposes it on us; it is the result of our interactions with the rest of the system.

How can we find out what this consensus is? This is not clear at all. In principle, one has to try to find out what society expects from us, but we can only really find out if we can filter out completely our momentary self-interest in the broadest sense of the word. It is not easy to discover where we are emotionally involved, a tricky question; the only thing one can say is that those with an immediate interest in an issue are disqualified, they are bound to be biased. For example, if you love your twenty-five-year-old Dodge, you are bound to come up with such justifications as no need for recycling, lower NOx, etc.

But the rest of us of course know that the twenty-five-year-old Dodge is: (1) too heavy, (2) too fuel inefficient, (3) too polluting (even if not in NOx).

Somewhere deep down, we all know that what we should go for is the small lightweight 75-mpg runaround. Now, here we touch the emotion of just about the whole of America and its love affair with the car. So in this area most of you guys are disqualified; it is the rest of the world who will have to tell you what responsible motoring is!

PAMELA McCORDUCK: Food for thought, Kees. I always start suspecting people who have the confidence to tell me what my responsibility should be. Yes, I am deeply attached to

that part of my autonomy, deeply and emotionally attached! I'll make a wild guess that I'm not the only one.

Give up my gas-squandering RX-7? The car I should have
had when I was twenty-five but couldn't then afford?

And more seriously, a lightweight 75-mpg runaround has
to share the highways with trucks of gargantuan size, at
least in this real world. One wouldn't have a prayer, come a
collision. I don't bike in Princeton, or in Berkeley, simply
because the roads belong to automobiles, though I understand all the advantages of a bike.

BARBARA HEINZEN: But would you lobby for bicycle paths
that compete with autos, or simply let someone else worry
about the problem? Presumably, as long as you had an auto,
bicycle paths are only a "good idea." Only when cycling
was a necessity would the lobby become useful.

STEVE BARNETT: I see a new kind of postmodern mysticism
here. Kees, are you using words like "culture" or "love affair
with cars" as final causes, to be invoked with no further
need of explanation? Why does this love affair persist?
Does culture throw out symbols and meaning in an endless
rich spew?

KEES VAN DER HEIJDEN: Management has very little discre-
tionary room for maneuver if it wants the corporation to
survive in a competitive marketplace. It requires continuous
diligence and there can be no slack in discipline. Management can never instruct the organization to do something
that is not good business.

Fortunately, if you are in it for the long run, corporate
responsibility is good business. I believe that all responsibility derives from a broad underlying consensus in society,
left after you strip out all the distorting individual direct
interests. It is the sort of view you see on these rare occa-

sions when you are totally at peace with the world, and when all your petty anxieties have moved into the background.

Clever companies try to be in harmony with this deep structure, because it is where society wants to be in the long run. But corporations also have their own little petty interests like all of us, and they have the same problem stripping these out from their observation filters. This is what they have to do if they want to discover their responsibility. Not everybody is equally effective in this.

KEVIN KELLY: Well said. Trying to pin down a quantifiable boundary on responsibility reminds me of *A Great Place to Work* (Robert Levering, Random House, 1988), a book trying to quantify the aspects of companies people loved to work for, which concluded that it had a lot to do with "trust," so that everyone from janitor to VP trusted the company. We probably don't want a responsible automobile. We do want a responsible automobile company.

PAMELA McCORDUCK: Won't one follow from the other?

BARBARA HEINZEN: Not if automobiles, per se, are irresponsible.

KEES VAN DER HEIJDEN: Pamela, I understand that you wish to decide this for yourself. Who does not? But look at it from one step up. Your choice will not be just a whim, I suppose. You will want to justify it to yourself. This is where my argument comes in. You can only reason out your relation with your environment by reference to the purpose of a larger system that encompasses both. But reasoning out this purpose requires a larger system still. And so on. Somewhere along the line, you have to refer to something outside yourself or you will never stop. It is my thesis that, whether we want it or not, our reasoning is always culturally determined. Mind you, even something as basic as the categories we think in is culturally determined.

Many people do not reason it out like that; they will refer to instinct or intuition. That is even more strongly tied to culture.

I cannot see how anybody can come to defining his responsibilities in society without referring somewhere to the broad stream of consensus that we call "culture." (Somehow I am not happy with the word "culture" here; paradigm or something?)

Steve, final causes need as much explanation as any other causes. Let me explain what I am struggling with. Responsible behavior is highly normative, if only to yourself. I am interested in where this norm comes from. Rather important, you know, if you want to explain to someone that he had better change his behavior. If people are less and less prepared to follow a central authority without questioning, it must have grown in consciousness through contact generally with society.

Also there must be something like an undercurrent here, separate from day-to-day fluctuations, otherwise we could never be aware of acting irresponsibly. All this seems self-evident to me. I am aware that I have not said very much more by bringing in words such as "culture." I think the question of emotion is important, though. I believe that strong emotion can interfere with a sense of responsibility. It causes mental activity in the here and now and temporarily decouples from the broad societal undercurrent. That is why those that are strongly emotionally involved should mistrust their judgment. Look at how we pick juries, etc.

RUSTY SCHWEICKART: What, then, is Kees's cultural norm for responsibility? Especially with respect to the automobile?

1

2

3

And are the rules of the game (corporate) compatible with the means by which such a cultural norm is established?

Seems to me that, re the automobile, we could list such qualities as safety, efficiency, durability, environmental cleanliness, and perhaps maintainability, as components of responsibility. I'm sure there are others—perhaps some aesthetic components.

But I suspect that corporate profitability (as Kees states beautifully) forces compromises in responding to these norms. Corporations realize full well that Pamela *will* buy the RX-7 she always wanted (as soon as she can afford it) despite the fact that both she and they understand the RX-7 is not consistent with the cultural norm of responsibility.

Fact: we do *not* act responsibly (much of the time) and we do not *want* to act responsibly. We want status, image, speed, comfort, and many other things that are not components of the responsibility norm. Therein lie the profits and the juice of the game.

PETER COYOTE: Kees, your point about "why" be responsible to anything outside yourself suggests one obvious answer: because, on some level, nothing is "outside"; the universe is absolutely interdependent and this principle always manifests itself. Who would have thought years ago that heroin dropped off in black neighborhoods as a pacifier would find its way into white suburbs? Who would have thought that the Shiite underclass could eventually throw the Israelis, Maronites, et al., out of Lebanon. Who would have thought that educational policies designed to keep people tractable by diminishing their analytical skills could have resulted in America's loss of manufacturing dominance? Who would have expected that racism in the employment opportunity division spawned crime as a major self-employment industry?

The model extends to plants and animals. A tree cannot live without sunshine, water, microbes in the soil, squirrels and voles to spread those microbes, truffles to grow them (eaten by the squirrels and deposited around the forest floor as fecal pellets which colonize fir-tree root hairs so that they can absorb minerals). Consequently one can say, absolutely strictly, that the tree has no separate existence from that with which it is interdependent. The illusion of a separate existence is the folly that powers nation-states, world religions, corporations to address themselves to limited audiences, creating ins and outs, or haves and have-nots, which invariably change places over time.

Furthermore, because of this interdependence, direct information comes to each of us over the spinal telephone, and if we sit quietly and cut off the chatter, we can each get clear and precise information about the nature of our relationship to the world around us, which produces feelings and impulses that are appropriate and apparently self-generated. (The whole question of "inside" and "outside" is actually beggared by taking interdependence all the way, but this is how it "feels" to everyday common sense.) These feelings, and minding them, produce autonomous, self-sustainable behavior that is very powerful. It is behavior which can and often does overthrow the status quo that is fueled by people who are basically taking orders. This is not to obviate cultural pressure as a determinant or obstacle to personal insight, but it is not the metasystem that is the most important. Many brave souls defied Nazism, for instance, to rescue Jewish friends and neighbors, putting their own lives at great risk. One could say probably that each and every great leader and prophet has been such a person. Your model of integrity-by-consensus sounds inherently corporate if I understand it correctly, and I would suggest just considering the opposite point of view a bit, and seeing if it doesn't yield some value in this discussion.

BARBARA HEINZEN: Unfortunately, there is a lot of noise/interference on the spinal telephone so that our ability to take the health of the planet as interdependent with our own health and long-term survival is often limited. What does it take to reduce the noise? Some of which (e.g., I must protect my family) can seem more immediate, and often is.

PAMELA McCORDUCK: Think I'll resist the opportunity to defend my squalidly selfish, victim-of-corporate-dupe decision to buy and drive an RX-7. [She added the symbol ":-"; in the world of electronic conferencing this symbol means a smiling face (look at it sideways).]

However, I am sensitive to the several sets of values which responsibility in general addresses, values that extend well beyond my own skin. Like Coyote, I firmly believe that we cannot accurately predict just what the results of our decisions will be in the long term (and often not even in the short term). We do the best we can and try not to be surprised when they come back to haunt us. What does it mean, to "do the best we can"? One thing I do is try and expose myself to the most outrageous opinions that I can, and I try to predict for myself which of them will be a "truth" that I will someday feel quite comfortable with. Defining responsible behavior is a cultural enterprise, and it is a consensual exercise, and I don't know why anybody would be surprised at either.

PETER SCHWARTZ: Kees observed that "Clever companies try to be in harmony with this deep structure, because it is where society wants to be in the long run." Is perhaps the commitment to the persistent search for that deep structure, and the attempt to harmonize with it, the most practical definition of "responsibility" that transcends particular cultures?

KEES VAN DER HEIJDEN: What else comes down the line through the spinal telephone besides the product of mental processing of a lot of input signals, which emanate from the culture around us, and particularly of feedback from this culture about our own actions?

Or, Peter, are you suggesting that there are other as yet not described communication lines at work?

JACK HUBER: Kees, is it possible for a corporation to be in tune with the deep underlying structure of responsibility and still sell "responsibility" through messages aimed at narrow segments of the market, similar to the efforts on the radio station in San Francisco? Can one modulate the day-to-day vibes with the low-frequency signals?

I don't know why but this discussion is beginning to remind me of Aunt Hill in *Godel, Escher, Bach.*

The concepts of the individual needs/wants playing off the needs of the total, and the idea of referenced or relational needs nested one within the other, suggests some kind of optimization game. So who optimizes and what's the game? Kees's point on corporate profit seeking for long-term survival is taken . . . in today's nesting of relationships. What is the higher authority to change the referencing mechanism? Is it government—in an era of globalization? Is it the "total"—whatever that is, and however it can be monitored?

Many would say individual transportation is suboptimized today. But with respect to what? The idea of resonating with an underlying frequency is appealing, even if using it for commercial purposes also appears crass—if it puts us all in tune and leaves the illusion of independence. Is this really a systems problem?

3

The Consumer's Responsibility

●

PAMELA McCORDUCK: Certainly the issue of drunk driving hinges on explicit codification. It isn't a matter of whether you think you're capable (or if you are) but whether your blood level shows a certain level of alcohol. We have no comparable way to measure emotional distress, absent-mindedness, or other states of mind that would make one an irresponsible driver, and so we do not have laws against these.

DON MICHAEL: Ah, Pamela, you've opened up another Pandora's box (or maybe another compartment in that commodious contribution to our multiple plights). If drinking drivers have so little inclination to caution about the future of their own well-being, their family's, or that of the other folks on the road, why should we expect them to feel responsible about contributions to something so far in the future or so abstract as the environment or the greenhouse effect or the ozone layer?

They don't need to be able to know they are drunk. All

they need to know is that, *not* knowing whether their driving might be impaired, they should, if they are responsible, designate another driver, etc. Seems to me this is analogous to taking responsible precautions about the greenhouse effect.

Recall that people avoid speed limits by using radar monitors, and were/are so resistant to seatbelts that laws are required to get a reasonable level of compliance. Too irresponsible to use them otherwise.

If one assumes (and I do) that in this frustrating world more people will drink and use drugs, then perhaps cars need to be designed to be immovable if the driver breathes out alcohol residues, and laws need to be passed to make this profitable for auto builders, just as with seatbelts.

KEES VAN DER HEIJDEN: Don, I do not think I know any people who are in favor of drunk driving. The drunk driver will another day completely agree with you that drunk driving should not be allowed. This is the same as Catherine's "One clue: many people who do not individually make responsible choices will vote for legislation that will enforce responsibility."

This is the distinction that we need to make between the general principles which most of us can subscribe to (in moments when we are not personally involved) and our immediate personal interest in an actual day-to-day event, which at that moment may well make us take an opposite decision. I like to think about it as the broad undercurrent, changing only slowly and forming the foundation of our legal system and public morals, and the high-frequency noise as that which cannot be the basis of anything because it will be different tomorrow. If we knew how to filter the two, we would have solved the responsibility problem.

4

Can Anyone Afford to Take the Long View?

●

KEES VAN DER HEIJDEN: What constitutes responsible behavior depends a lot on the time scale you value. Our problem is that there is only one market in society where we put a numerical value on the future, and that is in the cost of capital. As there is no other number available, this one becomes terribly influential. And it is not future-friendly.

Anything that happens twenty years from now or later has negligible effect on current decisions, according to this measure (roughly speaking). Can we escape its tyranny? It is all very well to say, "I know better; I will take a different line," but in this market world this is only a recipe for extinction.

STEWART BRAND: Kees's pointing at time scale being pinched by the complete dominance of return on capital I find completely persuasive, plus the deferral to government as responsible for the long term.

But it is bigger corporations also that we look to for

taking the long view, especially in a time of fading governmental puissance.

JOHN ROZSA: If I were a corporation looking over our attempts to define what responsible means and what implica-
tion it might have for the kind of product I was going to
manufacture, I would be very concerned about making very
large commitments in the near future. What would make
me cautious would be:

1) the possibility that environmental enthusiasm might be a
very transitory phenomenon among the buying public that
I need to cater to; and

2) that public uncertainty about how much responsibility is
enough would leave my customers vulnerable to other vehicle attributes such as performance as their basis for deciding
what to buy.

Given the above, I would ask, "What is the best, least
risky way for me to demonstrate through my product's
characteristics my company's commitment to more environmentally aware vehicles?"

I think that the short-term answer to this question is that
you can't do much to your actual vehicles now. You can
begin to engage in R&D and start to publicize it so as
to accrue benefits to your image as a responsible corporation.

In the long run, you have to begin to involve yourself in
the regulatory changes that will come, to make sure that
you can help define what is needed. For example, suppose
Los Angeles instituted an ordinance that prohibited cars
which did not have certain characteristics from entering the
central city. If your research showed that nothing could
compete, from a cost and environmental standpoint, with
low-powered, petroleum-fueled ultralight vehicles, you

would want to create a central-city environment that complemented such vehicles.

DON MICHAEL: Consider, too, that most people seem to live in the present, if we assume that the TV news people correctly interpret their audiences' perceptual preferences (71% of Americans get all their news from TV). And what does advertising appeal to? Instant gratification. Tomorrow's product today. And then there is the simple matter of living out the current twenty-four hours satisfactorily, an increasingly challenging task for harried, overworked, worried folks. "Just try to find time for quality time," they tell me.

So, is there much room for a serious place for the future in most folks' definition of responsibility? And what events, messages, models might change that? If I were in business or were a politician, dependent on a lot of customers/constituents, I would want to know about that.

KEES VAN DER HEIJDEN: In our market world, even the most responsibility-oriented company cannot escape the tyranny of the cost of capital. A company that wishes to survive cannot put a lot of weight on anything that happens twenty years from now. Something that will happen in sixty years' time (to pick a number) is irrelevant, and it would be irresponsible (read suicidal) to let it affect your decisions now. It is the law of survival in the marketplace, which nobody can escape. Only if it can be anticipated that the possibility of the sixty-year phenomenon will enter public awareness, such that there is a significant effect on behavior within the twenty-year frame, does it become of potential business interest.

STEWART BRAND: That's persuasive and gloomy. So . . . what is the logic of government taking a sixty-year view?

Winston Churchill used to argue that that's one good use of monarchies—their interest spans generations. And indeed the British royals have been exemplary on environmental matters. But they have no teeth, and monarchy is not coming back, so what does that leave for governmental long-term responsibility logic?

PETER WARSHALL: Classical, preindustrial humans had a time scale of five generations. Genuises like the Australian aborigines held seven to nine in mind as part of the oral traditions. In the Euro-American cultures, the time scale is from great-grandparent, grandparent, parent, ego, to children of ego. This is the human time scale that used to be the arena for strategic planning. The postindustrial demise of kinship linkage went hand in hand with the more narrow concerns about time and the community. The question of responsibility is, then: With the new family/kinship web, how is concern for grandparents or grandchildren to be defined? Do we want our kids to see spotted owls? What if a grandchild should prefer elephant watching to car manufacturing? Should he/she have that option?

5

Corporate Learning

●

CATHERINE BATESON: I said earlier that I would put in a comment about what I have been calling responsiveness.

Any organism acts not in response to external reality (whatever that may be) but in response to an internally constructed version of that reality after available information has passed through a series of filters. The most obvious filters are sensory; many organisms process sensory information not available to human beings without special equipment; others have sensory systems very narrowly adapted to particular needs. But human beings also filter through what we call attention and on the basis of what we call relevance.

Many years ago my father proposed that conscious purpose was maladaptive because, he argued, such purposiveness led to partial perception, not of full cybernetic loops but only arcs of those loops.

But, clearly, when you focus on the achievement of some particular defined purpose, you will sort through available information using some kind of criterion of relevance. Do tuna fishermen regard the demise of dolphins as relevant? Until recently, no. Interestingly, one effect of public relations is to change criteria of relevance. Because of the different governance structure in the Eastern bloc, pollution was not seen as relevant until recently.

So it would be possible to construct a number of ways of evaluating relevance criteria. We have talked about some of these. One of the most obvious is time depth—are outcomes five years down the line seen as relevant to decision making? (see "Can Anyone Afford to Take the Long View?" p. 131). Boundaries are important too, in the form of self-definition—whose welfare is part of the welfare of a particular corporation (many corporations support symphonic music)?

One of the very important filters we use is whether a dollar value—or some kind of numerical value—can be put on a particular factor. Let us take it as axiomatic that Nissan makes decisions for its own benefit—but what is its own benefit? What indeed constitutes survival?

Surely Nissan would suffer if the Japanese economy fell apart—but also if the U.S. economy or relations with Japan fell apart. Aha, enter the factor of threshold—issues that may be irrelevant most of the time may become relevant when they pass a certain threshold. Thus we can pose the question of responsibility in terms of "What do you take into account in your decision making?"

Next, however, we can ask whether a particular person or entity has what I have been calling peripheral vision—keeping the corner of your eye open for things that might prove relevant—and a habit of defining relevance very broadly. There is a sort of spectrum between narrow purposiveness and a more open responsiveness. Increasingly, people are being asked not to go do what needs to be done and do it well, but to meet narrowly defined criteria and to be blind to everything else. What is the conceptual change that would allow me to regard the survival of a species of squirrel or owl as relevant to my purposes? Nissan's purposes?

In the parable of the good Samaritan, the question is not how you treat your neighbor, but who is your neighbor? Relevance. And do you even notice what is happening on the other side of the street?

KEVIN KELLY: Catherine, I agree wholeheartedly with your keen insight about relevance thresholds. Those thresholds are dynamic, changing as the organism adjusts it own relevance to others. What is the process in which an organism becomes aware of other considerations? It's the same as asking, How do organisms learn?

What we are studying here is how corporations learn to be responsible. What we may be answering is that corporate learning in itself is the main element of responsibility. Dialogue as an instrument of response and learning as a prime tool. I see the way to making corporations more responsible as completing the half-arcs of communication and lines of control that are pointed to the levels of organization around them.

CATHERINE BATESON: Kevin, I think, strictly speaking, that a given relevance threshold might define a corporation as responsible at a given time, but learning would involve changes in the threshold. If Nissan set aside five minutes of every board meeting to discuss, e.g., the greenhouse effect, without committing itself to any given course, the structure of the discussion would change.

STEWART BRAND: That is a diabolical notion, Catherine, having a responsible body routinely discuss some issue for which no action is planned. But you know, and they know, that by bearing the issue in mind their actions will eventually reflect the consideration—maybe even better than direct action would.

Have you seen this tried anywhere?

KEES VAN DER HEIJDEN: Catherine has just written one of the best introductions to scenario planning ever:

1. An organism acts in response to an internally constructed version of reality.
2. Human beings filter through what we call "attention" and on the basis of what we call "relevance."
3. Relevance determined by time depth and boundaries of "self."
4. The notion of threshold value in relevance.
5. Conscious purpose is maladaptive, because it leads to partial perception.
6. There is a sort of spectrum between narrow purposiveness and a more open responsiveness (peripheral vision; do you even notice what is happening on the other side of the street?).

I would add to this the point that the internally constructed version of reality of an institution is a subset of those of its members, a sort of common denominator effect. I think this is related to threshold effects, thresholds being higher for institutions than for their individual members. This is why each institution has the capability of peripheral vision if it can mobilize the microcosms of its members. From what we discussed elsewhere in this conference, the Japanese culture may be better at this than the American culture.

I have found that many more perceptive managers wonder whether their corporate mental maps, their peripheral vision, might be too limited for this fast-changing world. Companies that stick with scenario planning have discovered it as a way of widening peripheral vision by reducing threshold values of institutional attention and relevance (e.g., they have discovered that you can have a highly successful scenario exercise while completely disbelieving all resulting scenarios).

Kevin suggests that corporate learning in itself is the main element of responsibility. If "responsibility" = capability to learn, I was wondering, does the Nissan management team engage in scenario planning?

6

Scenarios for the Next Millennium

●

DON MICHAEL: Pretend it is the year 2000. Then take some aspect of what has preoccupied you in our conference and create a bit of a scenario about its situation at that time. Presumably you will draw on what you have learned from others here, as well as upon your own speculations, to create your scenario.

It could be about corporate responsibility, or individual responsibility, or how cars are used, or what a responsible car is like—or *is* there a "responsible" car? It could be a wide-focus scenario about contending definitions of responsibility, for example. Or it could be narrow-focused; say, one person going out to buy (or rent or borrow) a car. Etc. It could be a scenario about the status of regulations relevant to transportation. Indeed, you might want, instead, to describe how some state of affairs got to where it is in 2000, by tracing it from now until then.

You can build your piece of scenario around whatever engages you out of our musings, seekings, arguings. These scenario fragments surely won't add up to a single coherent picture, but they could give us a better appreciation than we have now of what *different* world views might be constructed, or what different futures for responsibility (or the lack of it) and its expression in automobiles—or something else—might lie ahead.

DOUG CARMICHAEL: I fear the world will look more like it does now than any of us suspect, except a greater tolerance for systemic failures: military, political, ecological, medical (plagues because we are so tasty and ill defended). In this world, many will do well and most will do poorly. It won't show because personal angst will be hidden, as it is now, by the media's average view of the world which is so different from the world's average. Now, for cars. Plot the growth of the human population and superimpose the car population on this time line. Amazing, and add that the one thing we know that drives down human population growth rate is achieving middle-class status; the very thing that drives the car population. From an evolutionary perspective, we have met our mistletoe and it is our cars. Clever beasts, they really have a thing going, and show that mindlessness is no bar to success as a species.

BARBARA HEINZEN: In considering what scenarios might be for the year 2000, I thought to take it geographically and consider three types of environment: central London (specifically my neighborhood, Clerkenwell), a New York suburb on Long Island (where my parents live), and Cameroon (where I did my PhD fieldwork).

Clerkenwell:

The ideal in this neighborhood, currently filled with small workshops and public housing (75% of residents), would be to improve public transport and discourage auto transport. Public transport could be improved by opening an underground station at Mount Pleasant, halfway between Kings Cross and Farringdon Road, with links to Hackney, an area that has no underground service at all. Better bus routes along Clerkenwell Road and Rosebery Avenue, with the introduction of bus lanes to speed public transport, would also improve the area. Some sort of fee on private cars coming into central London should be introduced, with the funds so raised being put into public transport.

A growth in offices, which is likely, as we are on the fringes of the financial district, could also support more centralized shops and services in the neighborhood. This would, overall, reduce the need to travel for basic services. If this development does not take place, and if office growth is not introduced judiciously, we could have an overloaded road system. The increased auto traffic would eventually discourage investment in the area and force people and offices to move to more convenient locations.

Plandome, Long Island:

This tiny suburb of New York has a train station linking it to Manhattan, but no local shops and no local transport system. It is a wealthy neighborhood with fairly large houses and gardens. Everyone who lives here has at least one car and usually two or three. My parents have two cars and are in their late sixties. Apart from mailing a letter with a stamp already on it, nearly every chore requires a car: groceries, post office, library, drugstore, etc. The history of postwar development on Long Island has been one of virtually unlimited growth in middle-class housing, supported by public expenditure on roads rather than on rail or public transport. There has been little support for maintaining a "green belt" of any kind, or in any way defining a public, as opposed to a private, good. One scenario would see these values change, as individuals realize there are gains to be made by working to defend a greener environment and by encouraging the protection of those historic buildings that exist. (Some towns on Long Island were founded in the seventeenth century.) This scenario would include an increasing public pressure for more public transport and, possibly, changes in planning restrictions to allow for more small clusters of local shops in order to recentralize services around towns, rather than along roadways.

However, as local taxes are already quite high in the area, it is not clear that the investment will be made available for improvements in public transport. It is also likely that attempts to limit housing development and hence population will not succeed, since profits (and taxes) can still be raised by unrestricted growth. As a result, the area is likely to become overcrowded and unplanned, with an increase in private wealth amidst public squalor.

Cameroon:

Cameroon is a relatively small African country, with two or three existing and potential urban centers (Yaounde, Douala, Buea, Bamenda, N'kongsamba, N'gaoundere). The population is probably about 10 million people and growing. Cameroon has been relatively stable politically since independence and has also been a modest oil producer. It is a member of the "franc" zone and has strong links to France. It is very diverse ethnically, with a large number of linguistic groups living in a variety of ecological zones and supporting different kinds of agriculture.

One transport scenario for Cameroon would see the growth of rail links between the major town centers. This would help to unify the country politically and could reduce the need for private road transport. It would also have benefits in building the economy and could get substantial French backing, since railroads are a source of French pride. In this scenario, auto transport would grow more slowly and would probably be limited to local service. There is already a fairly good rail link between Yaounde, the capital, and Douala, the main port. (A responsible auto company might try to design "mini" containers to facilitate the links between long-distance rail and local transport of goods.)

The second scenario would see only limited investment in rail because of the inability to agree to a coherent transport policy and to raise the necessary investment money, on which there would be no immediate return. As a result, there would be increasing ad-hoc growth of road transport, with a need for vehicles capable of crossing poorly maintained and hazardous roads. There would be a considerable rise in pollution, since most of the fleet would be poorly maintained and usually secondhand, with low gas mileage. The development of a high-mileage, low-cost, rugged vehicle capable of transporting goods and people would be very valuable.

GRAHAM GALER: Before 2000 we shall probably have a United States of Europe, in all but name. It will provide federal government to the E.C., but the polity will be unlike any other that has so far existed (U.S.A., Australia, Canada, etc.). Much environmental legislation will be standardized across Western Europe, with the running made by Germany. Standards will be high and (by then) tightly enforced.

People will have tired of the endemic traffic congestion in and around cities such as Milan, Brussels, Paris, and London. Maybe also New York, San Francisco, Rio, Singapore, Sydney . . . Solutions will be found, mainly by way of cutting down traffic volumes (limited access, more pedestrianization, road pricing, etc.).

The age of mass tourism may be coming to an end, as people realize the irony of queuing for the Uffizi, suffocating in Yosemite, meeting nothing but other foreigners at Stratford-upon-Avon, and hanging around at airports when they are supposed to be "relaxing." Result—more differentiated travel, with perhaps greater use of cars and other recreational vehicles to get to quieter and more remote places.

Computer-mediated communication will have had another decade of experience and will be well entrenched. Discussion for such as this will no longer be avant garde, but common, in the academic, business, and professional worlds. Private citizens will be able to afford it too. This will lead to an explosion of trans-world communication, with complex consequences for car transport: more communicating from home, but more contacts, leading to more face-to-face meetings as well.

A final word on the scope for surprises. Not much more than a century ago, people were despairing of the growth of traffic in big cities. It was estimated that, if something didn't change, London would be several feet deep in horse manure by the year 1900. A big surprise—the internal combustion engine—came along, which led to the transformation of our streets and the loss of jobs by thousands of crossings sweepers. Are there surprises in store for us over the next ten or twenty years which will make all our present preoccupations seem unnecessary?

DON MICHAEL: The year 2000 is only eight years away for the U.S. as well as for Europe. But, whereas Europe has been revising its governance infrastructure for some years, we haven't even put together an energy policy. (After all, the U.S. has managed to ignore or reject many social and environmental policies which Europeans have sensibly practiced in recent years and longer; I doubt that we would suddenly see the light or be able to change our life ways quickly, even if we wished to.) So, in contrast to Graham's scenario about Europe, here is a very different one for the U.S.:

There are widespread frustration, anger, cynicism, and resignation with the social and economic burdens that seem to go on endlessly: traffic jams; social-welfare needs of the poor and middle class; crime; servicing the S&L costs and the national debt; deteriorating physical infrastructure; etc., etc.

There is repeated evidence of greed: outrageous inequities (e.g., gratuitous golden parachutes for dubiously deserving senior corporate persons); duplicity and deception in government and business, including misleading government reports and product descriptions. These are assiduously revealed by media diligently pursuing both responsible and irresponsible reporting, and by multiple contending public and private interest groups. In turn, attention, via certain media and interest groups, reveals irresponsible reporting by other media and interest groups.

As a result of our mal-education system, a very large part of the population, including many who have college degrees, is unable to understand the systemic complexity involved in resolving these burdens. Since solving them involves sacrifices, or at least substantial changes in life ways for many, and, thereby, threats to people's security in an already too threatening world, it is not in the interest of most politicians to encourage facing up to the issues. Since entertainment helps folks cope with their frustrations, there is no great incentive for many to seek exposure to the "facts" of life. And there is a large entertainment industry (including advertising) to aid and abet that disinclination.

Adding to all this is the widespread impression and, in many cases, the fact of loss of traditional boundaries from inside the person to the nation-state. It is less and less clear for many whom one is responsible to and what one is responsible for, in the absence of those traditional boundaries. Moreover, the attention-getting, entertaining examples of challenges and questions regarding responsibility are settled in the courts rather than by dependence on some "higher" inbuilt standards of what is right (which depended on the traditional boundaries of relations between persons and organizations and, indeed, within self).

All levels of government operate in a morass of status, conflict, and occasional experiment, but with no overall sense of where to go or how policy and programs should connect over time and circumstance. The pervasive changes in the composition of the judicial system, initiated during the Reagan presidency, mean that at many levels previous legal findings are reversed. Add to this, the U. S. Congress can no longer be expected to stick by its legislative actions. (First demonstrated decisively when it repudiated its 1989 landmark medical-assistance-for-the-aged legislation in 1990.) This means that different publics and businesses cannot expect ongoing reliability in policies and programs, or have any serious hope of getting decisive legislation, given intense conflicting public pressures. So, whether persons and businesses define their responsibility in traditional terms or in legal terms, there is a sense of mutability and confusion.

The result of these circumstances? A citizenry that, for this fragment of a scenario, can be roughly described as polarized into:

1) The portion insisting on more responsibility throughout the society, whether it be by following one's conscience, the commands of a deity, or by laws that establish ever tougher standards for conduct, product characteristics, and law and order. Members of this segment of society vary in their state of mind from aggressively militant, to downright smug, to deeply disturbed about the costs to civil liberties. But, one way or the other, they see the overriding priority as that of establishing and reinforcing standards of responsibility if there is going to be a civil society in the U.S. These people feel it is their responsibility to use products that embody responsibility, the more ways the better. Not

so seldom, this self-induced responsibility carries a freight of righteousness and a rewarding masochism which is derided by the larger portion of the population described below.

Among others, this causes problems for product producers who, out of their own sense of responsibility and/or desire to profit from this population, provide responsible products but don't want to sacrifice sales opportunities among the indifferent and the cynical, the other segment of the population. I describe it now:

2) The largest part of the population. They are confused by info-glut and by endless products to choose among. If they pay attention at all, they are angry at being constantly lied to in so many ways and so inconvenienced by the costs of living, monetary and otherwise. Most are cynical to the point of indifference. All they can really count on is being entertained. "Eat, drink, and be merry because, if I don't, someone else will, probably at my expense. So what the hell, I'm going to get mine, and I'm going to get it right now like everyone else. (And that includes a new air conditioner because the summers are so damn hot.) Besides, that's my right!"

The corporate members of this part of the population insist that to have it otherwise is to interfere with tried and true capitalism. The public is entitled to what it will pay for and "I'm in business to provide it."

In sum, this group asks, "Responsibility? Who needs it?"

Under these circumstances, it's hardly surprising that the U.S. in 2000 is a very uncivil society indeed. Nor is it surprising that conscientious corporations are cautious about committing themselves to products that would have their best markets in a civil—that is, responsible—society.

CHUCK HOUSE: Let us imagine three different "religious value sets"—those who believe in communication improvements to ameliorate poor conditions and spread word about efficacious solutions; those who believe in "order improvements," whether willed by concentrating upon procedure, upon automating certain societal functions, or upon environmental improvement; and finally, those who believe in "miracle cures," which might otherwise be termed "technological solutions." In groups that I am familiar with (i.e., have studied at some length) these three value sets are nearly mutually exclusive—that is, to believe in one value set is almost a priori to devalue or ignore possible contribution from another set.

There can be agreement among all three that they seek improvement in the bleak future specter, and none are cynical to the point of saying "To hell with others, I'll at least get mine." But they can and indeed strongly do differ in their view of what constitutes "better," and hence what they would perceive as "responsible" effort. The most concerning case for me, however, is the addendum observation in some groups that an additional complicating factor often arises. That is the Law of First Cousins, wherein all of those who share one value set differ substantially upon tactics by which to achieve the values sought. This, rather than the differing value sets, is so often in history what gives rise to internecine warfare, or civil war, or familial murder.

For example, among people who share the value set re communications, the group of first cousins would include those who favor computer teleconferencing; those who favor supersonic transport; and those who seek to revolutionize the post office; as well as the automotive equivalent of the NRA (is it the AAA?). Proponents of national policy to wire America (or the world) with fiber optic cable clash with those who want the 500,000 decaying bridges repaired. And so on.

Where this leads, of course, is to a paralysis of action precisely because so many routes are responsible, at least viewed from their sectarian value set. And I think it not inconsequential to observe that we can construct this kind of scenario more easily in America than in Europe (especially, Eastern Europe) because, as David Potter so aptly observed, we are a people of plenty. People with few options view any move as improvement; people with many options join the debate. And the debate may indeed be worthy from all sides, except the test of eventual result.

PETER WARSHALL:

SCENARIO FOR CARS AND RESPONSIBILITY:
A GUESS AT WHAT 2000 MIGHT LOOK LIKE

Cars must be considered from cradle and grave, to rebirth. That is, from Mining, Transport, Manufacturing/Assembling, Use, Reuse, and Discard.

MINING: By 2000, I see not much change. The industrialized world holds the purse strings of the undeveloped nations. The strip mining; downstream flooding; hill-slope slippage and pollutants caused by aluminum strip mining; noble metals extraction; iron-ore harvesting will remain relatively insensitive to environmental concerns. Undeveloped nations are more concerned with money than with "saving" the land.

TRANSPORT: Oil-spill control will improve, but not the severity or number of oil spills. In fact, oil companies will become more sophisticated in dealing with public relations,

1
5
1

not in dealing with long-term recovery of wildlife and oceanic resources from spills or accidents. The public is already getting used to the crisis scenario of spill-outrage-forgetfulness, which will be orchestrated a lot better than *Exxon Valdez*, without confronting major environmental and safety issues.

MANUFACTURING: There will definitely be a move toward flexible-fuel cars that may be tailored to the middle class and toward specific pollution "bubbles" such as L.A. or Tokyo. This will occur only in the industrialized world. In other areas, the same old same old. Subsidies and tax breaks and special maintenance contracts will help flex-fuel cars.

Despite higher energy and pollution costs, aluminum will remain a major material in cars. Petroleum plastics will stay because of lobbying and gas-mileage savings, despite the difficulty of recycling car plastic parts. This is an area with lots of enviro hype and conflicting information. If lucky, someone will figure out how to recycle some of the plastics and reduce the hidden cost of solid-waste management.

Catalytic converters dependent on noble metals will fade as the emphasis switches to preventive vs. curative methods of emission control. There will be no chlorofluorocarbons in air conditioners. More ceramics. No asbestos in brakes. Less rubber in tires and insulation.

FUELS: Methanol will increasingly enter the market, especially from 1996 on. Liquid petroleum gas and compressed natural gas will find small but stable niches in the market, especially in fleets. Ethanol and reformulated gasoline will lobby hard. Their success will depend more on lobbying than on environmental usefulness. Diesel-fuel research will improve emissions, claiming a better fuel to slow global warming. Global warming will be uncontrollable, and a minor issue compared to health. Energy security will not be a major criterion for lobbyists as fuels diversify.

USE: Use will not be dependent on any wholistic notion of environmental responsibility despite all the advertising to make consumers feel good about their purchases. Use will remain a complex of highway and construction business lobbying and of more general economics. The metropolitan-suburban commute will be constant and will rely on mass transit. The suburban-suburban commute will stimulate the sales of more cars. The extra-metropolitan business center to other centers will also stimulate more cars, especially multipurpose vehicles such as small pickups or suburbans.

The health lobby and the solid-waste-dump enviro concern will have the strongest impacts. The health lobby will call itself "enviro" and compromise with powerful economic interests in the regulatory theater. But the economic benefits of cleaner air in terms of health costs make this a powerful force. Solid-waste dumping (because of nonrecyclable cars) will cause heavier taxation and land-use conflicts for disposal, which will stir up passions.

The car will increasingly become tailored to each social group, from low riders to BMW-faxers. There will be lots of enviro hype as car manufacturers cite one aspect of their production and claim it shows how wonderfully responsible the company is. The major infrastructure of the car industry (parking, roads, etc.) will not change much, since this is a major labor lobby with lots of subsidies in the U.S. Japan and Europe will be different. In the U.S., parking rates will lead to more imaginative ways to car-pool, although the class difference between worker and upper-management parking remains unsolved.

The poor will get poorer and more populous and violate all attempts to limit use of gas guzzlers and polluters. The computerization of car mechanics will force the poor to stick to old, more easily repaired gas guzzlers or become more sophisticated break-in thieves for the computer-chip black market. Those who can afford it will remain highly righteous and insensitive. They will continue to ignore their behavior (driving) and become environmentalists by praising and seeking techno-fixes.

REUSE: There will be major industrial growth in recycling car parts that can compete with the use of virgin materials. This may influence the tire and plastic parts market significantly. Government help will stimulate this industry because of the impossibility of finding enough acres for landfill. Health problems in the recycling process (dusts, shreddings, etc.) will become a labor issue.

IN SUM: By the year 2000, congestion, air pollution/health, inner-city isolation from transport, fuel costs/energy shortages, and mass transit will not hurt the car industry. They will create tense shifts as new regulations that some car companies will profit by and others lose out on. "Responsibility," especially "environmental responsibility," will be used in any clever phrasing possible to try to sell more cars (make the consumer feel good about his/her purchase). But, compared to glitz, the environmental responsibility issue has little sex appeal, and cars must have sex appeal. The responsibility issue may help in specialty niches like the Volvo buyers.

Fewer and fewer people will believe that government regulations and corporate ethics can be consistent, reliable, compassionate, or accountable for health, safety, or the environment in a larger sense. Scandals, flamboyantly promoted to sell media, will become standard fodder that, indi-rectly, will maintain this cynicism and will justify consumer purchase of the latest car models no matter what their envi-ronmental impact. In fact, hypocrisy will become a pleasure in discussions of car purchases.

THE

BIG PICTURE

●━━━━━━━━━━━━━━━━━━━━━

1

Dealing with Events that Compromise a Corporate Reputation

●

PETER WARSHALL: Whew! I read the transcript after a weekend of searching for the last of the Mount Graham red squirrels and getting the news that Congress goofed in the wording of its law concerning the protection of the squirrel. Even though the Congress claims that they never wanted to stop the "process," the Justice Department claims that the language bypasses the Endangered Species Act. Since Congress is conveniently out of session, the representatives get to sound righteous and still allow the old-growth forest to be cut. These extralegal actions and convenient last-minute interpretations of the law (bulldozers waiting for the signal) is how I see speed, greed, and avoidance of responsibility (especially Mo Udall) integrating. Save face and let's plow ahead.

So let's get off the abstractions. Each person might give a case history of a particular responsibility dilemma. I remember Arie de Geus telling the story of Shell, Idi Amin, and

Uganda. The question was: Should Shell turn off the spigot? Should they cause the collapse of Amin's regime? Shell chose not to close the spigot. Was this responsible? Similarly, many corporations now face the apartheid question. Every corporation that does the "ecological" accounting will face difficult responsibility questions. Let's hear a few personal accounts. As Kevin Kelly says, how did you and/or your corporation learn to be responsible? Was the word ever used?

CHUCK HOUSE: Here's a case history. My dad was a car-driving traveling salesman, driving between 80,000 and 100,000 miles a year in low-mileage years, half again as much if times were lean. He bought a new car every 100K miles, so we had twenty-two new cars at home during my growing-up years. He drove fast, taught me a love of cars and a respect for them. But the point is, my dad used cars, and that is today how both my wife and I use transportation.

I have logged 1.2 million miles on United Airlines in the past four years, driven some 220 cars some 187,000 miles in that time, plus used my own company car (actually four cars) for another 45,000 miles. I don't own a car myself. I've also ridden a fair share of trains, subways, rickshaws, and other contrivances. The point is, I'm long past doing this for the love affair, or to play low rider, which is what 80% of my La Habra high school gang did.

I also know to some degree the ecological side, having served on Colorado's air-pollution commission for two years and done the EPA study on emphysema and high-altitude-emissions correlation in the seventies.

If you can do my job (and that of many others without cars, et al.), I'd be indebted. But it seems to me that the real freedom of cars is not for Suzy Housewife to run to the store, but for all of us to conduct our lives in vaster, more interconnected ways on a global basis. Granted that Joe and Suzy Six-Pack don't view it that way, but I'd imagine that many of us use four times as much fuel per year in our total world impact as the kids dragging Main Street in *American Graffiti*.

STEWART BRAND: Chuck, I wonder how you might view my slightly heretical view about electronic communications . . . namely, that the further burgeoning of electronic communications (such as this right here) will not diminish physical, energy-driven travel but increase it. Reason: convenient electronic communication, like this, gives people ever more colleagues and friends located in physically distant places with whom one wants, eventually, to have face-to-face contact—for closer work, for conference, for negotiation, or for friendship.

CHUCK HOUSE: Electronic communication, indeed, will lead to more rather than less physical communication. I agree, Stew, but the real excitement is how much more than could really be done face to face can now be done in advance, off-line, so to speak, and then face to face is used more for the value reconnection, the trust-factor rebuilding, the shared bonding of the physical association (I think). Edward Lias's book, *Future Mind*, talked to these points well— cameras created movies; movies created videotapes; but cameras and movies flourished later rather than shrank, even though there was a brief fallback.

DONELLA MEADOWS: Here's an example, to my mind, of corporate responsibility. In the mid-seventies, just after the first oil price rise and before the second one, Volvo commissioned its most creative car designer, Rolf Mellde, to design a car that would provide the freedom to move around, to live in a wide area, to visit friends, to live a richer life, but that also would minimize energy use during production, over the lifetime of the vehicle, and even when it was scrapped. This cradle-to-grave concern with energy was a degree of responsibility at least a decade ahead of the times. (Nowadays, to be a decade ahead, I'd add a concern for hazardous-waste production at every stage, and I'd eliminate the concept of scrapping by insisting that every part of the car be easily recyclable.)

Mellde and his team came up with a two-passenger car with generous luggage space called the LCP-2000. It gets 100 mpg on the open road. It has a 3-cylinder direct-injection diesel engine that can burn ordinary diesel fuel or vegetable oil, thereby making no net impact on the greenhouse effect (if the oil source is grown sustainably).

The car is 26% steel, 23% aluminum, 32% plastic, and 7% magnesium. In spite of those high-energy metals, the car saves so much on mileage that its lifetime energy use would be about half that of present commercial high-mileage cars. It meets all U.S. safety and environmental regulations and is as crashproof as any other Volvo.

Now here's an example of corporate nonresponsibility: Volvo shelved the LCP-2000 project in 1983, when it had just four of these cars running. Its reason for not pushing forward was "lack of consumer demand," meaning oil prices were beginning to fall. Most other auto manufacturers also have viable 100 mpg cars waiting in the wings. (I know for a fact that Toyota, Peugeot, and VW do, anyway.) Meanwhile U.S. manufacturers are pulling out all the political stops to prevent the government from raising the current fleet mileage standard above 27.5 mpg.

Seems to me responsibility is the same thing, whether it's exerted by a corporation or a person. It's acting for the largest possible benefit, within the largest possible boundary—and, since we never act with perfect knowledge, it's being alert for negative results of our actions and being willing to clean up those negative results as much as possible. In short, it's being aware, alive, and participating in the total system for the welfare of the total system.

For a manufacturing company, it seems to me, that translates into awareness of, and responsibility for, the material, energy, and pollutant flows generated by the product— mine to dump, forest to incinerator, cradle to grave. It means awareness of the welfare of workers and customers. It means zeroing in on the real social need—comfortable mobility, not necessarily with cars—and serving that need, always to the best of one's economic and technical and organizational ability. According to the principles of "right livelihood," it means taking the focus off the profits, the market share, even the viability of the corporation, and putting the focus on filling a true social need. If the need is filled, the profits, market share, and corporate viability will manifest effortlessly. To sacrifice any degree of human or environmental welfare to purely economic ends, or to the perpetuation of any particular corporation, is to get everything exactly backward. People need mobility; they don't need the continued existence, much less the growth, of Volvo or GM, or Nissan.

I think everybody should read again the chapter on "Buddhist Economics" in E. F. Schumacher's *Small Is Beautiful.* He makes responsibility sound very simple. Which, I think, it is.

163

2

Who Will Lead the Environmental Movement?

●

ART KLEINER: After spending a few months researching the current turnaround on environmental issues, I've come to believe that it's several trends happening simultaneously. One is relatively slow and deep and has to do with sustainable development. Another, also somewhat slow and deep, combines concern for global warming with the feelings that Earth First!-type people may have a point. Then there's the faster, maybe more evanescent, perception about green consumerism.

CATHERINE BATESON: The same forces that have recycling bins popping up all over the country have Nissan worrying about responsibility. But do small incremental and symbolic changes add up to real change—or how can they be encouraged to do so?

Barry Commoner used to point out that the only really definitive improvements were achieved by banning, not by reduction (i.e., DDT and atmospheric testing).

ART KLEINER: I just did an article for *Garbage* magazine on the reasons for the new wave of corporate environmentalism itself—I was trying to find specific factors and found several:

1. The tangible evidence of global warming and the tangible provability of emissions in water (through comparatively recent advances in measuring devices) make it harder to deny dire effects.
2. Perceived benefits from energy efficiency and from selling waste materials. (Monsanto reportedly saved millions this way.)
3. Fear of regulation, now that executives can be thrown in jail for knowingly covering up pollution, and now that at least one court (in Texas) allows civil suits by victims of pollution-related medical hazards from other countries.
4. Worker participation. (Workers tend to be environmentally conscious because the plant affects their health and neighborhoods.)
5. Green consumers. And corporate people getting sick of bad P.R.
6. The Brundtland idea of sustainable development made a significant difference. No longer did companies feel that they had to give up growth in order to be environmentally conscious.
7. Baby-boom-aged environmentalists finally reaching the point where they have enough power or support within companies to come out of the closet.
8. No one wants their beach-front property to be submerged by rising oceans.
9. Environmentalism and waste management may be a big-growth business for companies that are looking for big-growth businesses—particularly chemical companies, which are learning to do this sort of thing anyway.

10. If every chemical company has to keep up with strict regulations, that keeps upstart newcomers from entering the business. Thus, no chemical company wants to be first with a new technique, but once one company is forced to use it, they want all the companies to have to do it.

KEES VAN DER HEIJDEN: Could I suggest that there is a fundamental difference between general pollution and overcrowding problems, and the one in particular called "climate change." It will not do to put these together on one heap. If it were not for climate change, one could reasonably hope for society to find a technical fix in all problem areas we have been discussing here, without fundamentally changing what we want to do. Climate change is different, because it has this one-to-one relation with the absorption capacity of the planet which cannot be altered by any fix. If we want to envisage the car of the future, look for minimal impact on climate. The rest will come one way or the other.

BARBARA HEINZEN: I take your point. The issue we most want to avoid is that we are living with a finite natural-resource base and must cut our cloth accordingly

KEES VAN DER HEIJDEN: The book that made me understand why climate change is so difficult to handle for the corporate sector is David Pearce's little book, *Climate Change, Meeting the Challenge.*

3

Learning to Think Ahead

●

STEWART BRAND: I would like to see our culture be less pissy about people who were right early on. Retroactive respect would encourage other people to essay being right early. Surely, companies who are the first to identify and come down on the right side of a responsibility issue gain a certain competitive advantage. The most conspicuous current example is Star-Kist Tuna, which reversed itself suddenly on the dolphin issue and won relatively big—their competitors had to tag along, getting the disadvantages of the new policy but none of the credit.

DON MICHAEL: "Retroactive respect": great term, Stewart!

I wonder if those who are right early don't suffer from the same negative reactions as do whistle blowers? Whistle blowers are pointing to consequences—outcomes—and once one starts doing that, God knows what this will do to one's comfortable life.

PAMELA McCORDUCK: Retroactive respect—does it work? Yes, for a little while, but does it work for long? I have myself been "correct early" on one or two issues, and got beans for it. (I wouldn't have done it differently; I merely point out that the only reward for virtue is itself.)

DOUG CARMICHAEL: Do we have any historical examples of a society or part of a society becoming "responsible" about a major activity that was out of control? If so, can we learn from it; if not, what does that teach us about the way human communities use feedback?

4

The Hierarchy of Responsibility

●

PETER SCHWARTZ: As a civilization, I think we have focused on the morality of intentions, rather than on the morality of outcomes.

PETER COYOTE: I am confused as to the hierarchy of values implied by "responsibility." Are we responsible first to the species, human comfort, good business, the health of the planet, or what? I opt for long-term habitation of the planet as the best mechanism for affording us the time to sort out the other diddly. So until we agree about what we want or consider optimum, or what the spectrum of such possibilities is, I don't understand what we are speaking about.

A corporation, as I understand it, is responsible to its stockholders. It considers the community, the culture, et al., as the source of revenue that eventually supplies wealth to those stockholders. It makes calculated risks, like Ford deciding that it was cheaper to pay off deaths caused by design flaws in the Pinto than to retool the whole line and correct the flaws.

JOHN ROZSA: I agree with your characterization of corporations, Peter. They set themselves up to have limited liability (read, limited responsibility) for the same reasons that most of the rest of us establish contracts to govern our relationships with others (e.g., marriage contracts, the infamous prenuptial agreement). Two reasons: limited rationality—no matter how much we think we know what the future will bring, we really don't; and opportunism—our experience shows that people will take advantage of situations that benefit them at other people's expense. Any model that proposes to address all social quadrants simultaneously needs to explicitly confront these realities.

BARBARA HEINZEN: Which is to say, how do we make policy decisions that can balance all competing interests? What are the organizational forms, the rules of the game? You are suggesting, Coyote, that present rules don't work.

PETER COYOTE: Until government policy establishes targets, everything will continue in the same destructive hodgepodge fashion it does today. So what I am arguing out with you (or attempting to) is what the target of policy should be.

RUSTY SCHWEICKART: Peter Schwartz says we, as a society, have focused on moral intention rather than moral outcome.

1. Nothing wrong with intentions. Usually they're higher than actual behavior. The trick is to enable the reality to more closely approach the good intentions, whether by technological innovation or other means.

2. In my old California Energy Commission (CEC) days, we shifted the concept of the electric utility from that of a supplier of metered electrons to an "energy service corporation," largely by regulation. We insisted that the "real" re-

sponsibility of the utility was to provide the services the public wanted from electricity, not the electricity per se. This resulted in "forcing" the utilities downstream of the meter, into people's homes. Mostly into their attics (providing insulation), but also into their refrigerators (buying up old inefficient ones), along with other imposed regulatory insults. The result was a fairly dramatic improvement in energy efficiency in the homes of California.

The incremental "quantum" of available corporate responsibility in this instance was due to several factors:

1. the regulated/regulator juxtaposition;
2. the narrow vs. wholistic conceptual situation; and
3. the inefficiency embedded in the preexisting system.

In the case of nonregulated auto manufacturers, it looks like no. 1 doesn't apply, no. 2 may very well apply, and no. 3 certainly does.

In the marketplace, the available quantum of responsibility in no. 3 must be captured by innovation which is both attractive to the consumer and profitable to the producer. Could a shift in concept, from auto producer to personal-transportation provider, open some new possibilities for the industry?

STEWART BRAND: What were the downsides of the CEC intervention in the utility's business, if any? How has it been playing since your time in Sacramento?

RUSTY SCHWEICKART: I can only answer the first of your questions, Stewart, since I haven't kept direct tabs on what's happened since I left state government. I might get a quickie appraisal from my old sidekick Dan Richard, who has remained in the business.

As to the downsides of regulatory intervention, however, I would imagine that, from the industry (utility) point of

view, it was the forcing of a different role from their classical function. It was far simpler for an electric utility to
simply generate electrons, ship them down the wires
through the household meters, and send the public a bill.
But the systemic inefficiencies implicit in this arrangement
were (and in most states still are) economically punitive to
the customers and destructive of the environment.

There are two key points I would note here:

1. There was a confluence between the customer's paying too
   much and the unnecessary environmental burden, i.e., no
   difficult trade-off between environmental responsibility and
   consumer economic benefit.
2. There were very clear structural inefficiencies in the system,
   e.g., allowed rate of return based on capital investment
   (hence, incentives to build nuclear power plants and other
   capital-intensive systems).

In nonregulated industries, these conditions are not as prevalent.

By the way, in my thinking at the moment, it is point
No. 1 above which is where the crunch will come in century twenty-one. For the moment, whether we're dealing
with ozone, greenhouse, or whatever, there is sufficient
confluence between environmental insult and economic
inefficiency (from the consumer viewpoint, at least) that we
can make substantial progress without encountering too
many land mines. However, in a short time I think we'll be
into the fundamental confrontation between economics and
environment. Which is then to be the master and which the
slave?

PETER WARSHALL: There are regulations over each aspect of
the car's life cycle and they are changing (slowly perhaps)
to a more wholistic view of autos. They will first, since it's

easiest, attack the inefficiencies of the automobile—better catalytic converters, reformulated gasoline, methanol additives, lighter-weight vehicles, etc. This is already in process.

NANCY RAMSEY: Given the lack of public consensus on what targets and/or policy should be, "policy" is in fact (and all too often) hammered out in individual pieces of legislation and adjusted in later court battles or amended legislation. This leaves the formulation of public policy and the law to those who focus on it, working with lobbyists or otherwise. Unpleasant and imperfect as that may be, it is reality and it is increasingly true across the globe.

PETER COYOTE: I like to stress this notion of policy, because personal experience has demonstrated to me that the political process does not like it, precisely because it affords limits and says no to certain options and (more importantly) interests.

A brief example: I have (illegal) halogen headlights on my car. My high-beams are 60 watts (normal is 40) and, to go on the desert, I can insert a simple bulb from the back and raise them to 90 watts. They are illegal precisely because they are lobbied against by the makers of sealed-beams, who use old arguments from the 1930s about the dangers of nonsealed-beams in order to justify the exclusion of a superior and safer product. (Isn't this protectionism or something close to it?)

Until we can clarify some goals and begin to argue about the best ways to implement them, we're just a bunch of smart people throwing around our opinions for our hosts to glean for their benefit. (The point perhaps?)

It would be interesting to see if a small subgroup like this could ever reach something like consensus about goals and begin work on policies that might eventually offer guidance or pressure to the powers-that-be. That's why I'm hanging in there.

BARBARA HEINZEN: We have always valued the individual choice over the collective (or policy) choice, which involves balancing as wisely as possible a variety of competing interests. One can list all the historical reasons for that (immigrant nation running away from constricting societies, wide-open spaces, etc.), but we are running up against the social and ecological limits to that approach and need political forms that are capable of agreeing on a sensible, collective policy.

PAMELA McCORDUCK: I agree with Peter Coyote that for us as a small group to reach a consensus about goals is a fine idea. Then, some expression of policies toward those goals. And that's why I agreed to participate and am still here.

PETER WARSHALL: In my work, if this is helpful, we talk about three combos of power-desire-goals: INCENTIVES are the nicest. You keep public transport fares low in order to provide an incentive to use them. DISINCENTIVES are not so nice, require power and enforcement. These include congressional control over highway funds, now tied to air-quality standards, or traffic tickets for drivers whose cars don't meet exhaust standards, etc. The world is full of them. PERVERSE INCENTIVES are laws or money or policies that encourage something we don't want or which harms us. The federal subsidies of agribusiness water totally discourage healthier food production, for example.

In discussing responsibility, I think we should focus on these three distinctions. You can be responsible by advocating and encouraging incentives; by thinking up new disincentives and ways to enforce them; or by fighting perverse incentives. Each has its pleasures and anxieties. Personally, much can be done in corporate life by removing perverse incentives such as weird discount rates or strange alchemical models of internal rates of return (any accountants out there?). Many corporations are trying the incentive path with mixed results: Perrier blew it, there are no really recyclable plastics, etc. But it's a good path to think through. Perhaps those in this conference who are within a corporation should make a list for themselves, or for us, of the incentives, disincentives, or perverse incentives they would like to see encouraged or changed.

JIM PELKEY: I think we have to take into account the general behavior of systems to protect and continue existing behavior rather than change. Can the emerging awareness of critical environmental issues unfreeze our systems to allow reformulation of goals and rules? Is it realistic for that to happen before there is the preponderance of agreement as to the crisis or before an unparalleled disaster happens?

Thoughts: limit the energy use of an individual (annual ration?); encourage distributed work environments to cut down on transportation requirements; reward those who live on local resources; tax all consumption; and rebate to those (corporations and individuals) who practice desired behavior. . . .

DOUG CARMICHAEL: My first cut at the issues: we need a target plan, say, fifteen years, and phases, with specifics on how to get there. The conflicts that prevent a consensus are:

1. The desire for a car that can be disposed of vs. desire for a car that endures, so that cars on the street reflect new and healthier technology faster.

2. The desire for perks in our cars: fun, music, whatever.

3. The nagging suspicion this will be a rich-world scenario, not a full-world scenario, and that the conflict will overwhelm us at some point with a catastrophe.
4. A desire for a car-free world, some other culture, some other path.
5. Third-world car production and use could overwhelm any developed-world restraint.

KEES VAN DER HEIJDEN: The most important incentive we need to make responsible behavior possible is the internalization of externalities. Only governments can do that, as Adam Smith already pointed out. And government will act only under our pressure. Rather than telling a car company what "responsible" behavior is, maybe we should go and tell this to our politicians.

Or maybe there is a message for the car company here also: "We do not want you to go and counterlobby against the internalization of externalities." Maybe, in the final analysis, responsible behavior for the car company means not resisting the broad societal trend for the purpose of gaining some short-term profit.

JACK HUBER: Governments traditionally set the rules of the game for all players so that responsibilities don't get sandbagged by irresponsibilities. Corporations, even the biggies, play by the rules just like us—sometimes well, sometimes poorly. Driven also by another set of rules which define them, they influence government rules like we do. Joe and Sue [Six-Pack] and Sonja and Eric [Perrier] vote on who plays best—who delivers what they want, within the rules. Courts referee.

DON MICHAEL: The sum of my experience, as a sometime professional social psychologist, is that an awful lot of people don't "decide" in a self-conscious manner about much of anything. They act unreflectively, habitually, on the basis of peer style, belief, want, whim, feeling. They are not reflective unless confronted in one way or another, and then they still react in ways that have little to do with the semantics implicit in the verb "decide"; i.e., reasoned choice. This is one reason why "responsibility" is not, generally, a conscious consideration in shaping people's behavior. That requires standing outside of themselves and "objectifying" their situation. This is a disciplined way of being, which neither our educational experience nor our advertising context encourages for the most part.

As such, this is a major reason why we do have laws: to codify responsible behavior, to compensate for the ignorance and indifference of so many.

What can happen, then, is that if one is prudent, or believes in doing what the law says regardless or for various other reasons (as clarified by Kohlberg's work on levels of morality), law-compliant behavior becomes habitual, and then values shift to be consonant with behavior (e.g., the effect of the desegregation laws). This is not what the Enlightenment myth says about the democratic society, but there is much to argue that the myth is wrong.

Which says to me that we need more laws, well made and discriminating. So, as Kees proposed many comments ago, we need help from our responsible corporations, as we have defined them, to help us get such laws and to help block lobbying by those with a different set of motives and perspectives.

CATHERINE BATESON: On Don Michael's proposal, notice that maternal responsibility for children after birth is still working pretty well. But imagine a situation in which a substantial number of mothers said, "I'm not going to do this," as many fathers now do. Would the community pick up the slack, as it has gradually done for health and aging? Would maternal responsibility be enforced by some other sanction than the threat of the child being removed? Would increased codification work, and would it undermine residual responsibility or reinforce it?

Perhaps what I am saying is that this conference is not about responsibility but about achieving or preventing changes in people's unstated assumptions or stated obligations.

One case history to add, though I don't know the details, is fur. I have the impression that the campaign to make fur socially unacceptable has worked very well on targeted species, and with a spillover on ranched species, which I personally find no more unacceptable than breeding animals for meat or leather. I suspect that wearing a leopard-skin coat was once as delightful, as ego-enhancing, warm, sensuous, etc., as driving some of these vehicles described. But nowadays, anyone who even inherited such a coat from the old days could only dare enjoy it in an air-conditioned basement. Along with a cigarette.

STEWART BRAND: Dead on, Catherine. Environmentalists have been at their most effective in manipulating taboos. Second most effective: codified procedures such as environmental impact reports.

5

Legal Liability

●

JOHN ROZSA: Isn't our use of the word "responsibility" in connection with organizations an inappropriate anthropomorphism? Corporations are fictitious legal entities designed to limit the liability of their owners. Limited liability and responsibility seem an incongruous match.

BARBARA HEINZEN: Limited liability and responsibility, defined in the broadest terms, are definitely an incongruous match. Which is probably why this conference is necessary, because the limits on liability are being willy-nilly pushed further and further out.

PETER WARSHALL: I would like to say that "liability" and "responsibility" seem totally wired together. The corporations most involved are the insurance companies. First, the major liability cases have been environmental health and harm (asbestos, Agent Orange, oil-spill recovery). Can an insurance company take on certain liabilities just as they do with fire insurance? If so, then insurance companies will define—more than any other societal organization—what is "responsible" corporate behavior. They will set required standards for corporations which want insurance against health or environmental damage.

Note that nuclear power companies could never receive insurance policies, so the taxpayer, through congressional law, acts as the insurance agent. This favored status of the nuclear industry is a major reason that it exists. If you want a goal, remove the congressional insurance subsidy to nuclear power and watch the industry collapse or change drastically.

ART KLEINER: One book I can't stop thinking about is *The Suicidal Corporation,* written by Paul Weaver, who is now (I believe) at the Hoover Institute at Stanford University. Weaver was a dyed-in-the-wool member of the new right who went to work for Ford Motor Company in the early 1980s, leaving academia to see what it would be like to practice "pure capitalism." He ended up feeling that most of the Ford executives had betrayed pure capitalism in favor of "corporatism"—that most of them were seeking a welfare state, with themselves as the beneficiaries.

Perhaps that will not come as a surprise to anyone, but I found the specifics of his disillusionment fascinating. For example, he was in Ford PR during the Pinto episode. Says the Pinto got a bum rap; it was no more dangerous than other cars of the period. But Ford did not do the honorable thing: withdraw the car, investigate, defend itself, reintroduce the car. Instead it kept the car on the market and stonewalled. Its silence made people suspect the car.

6

Cars and the Third World

●

KEES VAN DER HEIJDEN: Are corporate boundaries disappearing or are they changing? I would say the latter, faster and faster. That's why we are having this conversation—new boundaries, therefore new responsibilities.

This question is becoming more difficult as the boundaries are moving further away and the systems are larger. The planet has become visible. The European-American culture base itself is no longer enough; we have to think of all the others too. We are searching for this much broader undercurrent. This requires conversation, as we are doing here.

What do you think is the "responsible" car, American or global?

JOHN ROZSA: Kees, we never handled responsibility well under the old boundaries. The new ones, if in fact there are any, throw people together in a superficial way—for example, via a common medium—but do not reckon with the different aspirations that people bring with them from their

old boundaries. Now we are proposing, in a way, that corporations via their products unify peoples as consumers—
perhaps replacing the brotherhood of man (no sexist reference intended) with the brotherhood of VCR owners.

Incidentally, I think the "responsible" car (if it's even a
car) is a developed nation's car, not a global car.

PETER GLEICK: There have been several comments so far that,
for better or worse, we live in an "automobile" society.
What seems to be missing from this argument is a vision of
the future. I'd like to argue that the idea of an automobile
society like ours, extended to the rest of the world, produces an impossible, unacceptable world because of limits
on resources and the ability of the planet to absorb environmental insults. The U.S. is responsible for emitting 25%
of the total annual global CO_2 burden, a third of which
comes from transportation. In California, nearly 70% of our
CO_2 emissions come from cars.

Question: Is it "responsible" to sell the automobile as now
designed to the rest of the world? [It is not responsible] to
the future, the environment, or society.

CHUCK HOUSE: My "reading" of the world scene is that we
have just begun to see the pressure of the Third World (or
the non-car-driving world) entering an automotive age. In
Eastern Europe, India, and China, people want the same
personal freedom and mobility all of us have "enjoyed."
This is even after seeing Lisbon, Madrid, Milan, and Paris
in gridlock. Taipei *wants cars.*

Would the responsible company say, "No, you shouldn't
have 'em, because we now know about the ozone-layer
problem"? Methinks of the Surgeon General's reports and
the exportation of the Marlboro Man to foreign lands.

Should we say, "Well, how about an urban transit sys-

tem," sort of like we did with Austria's digital phone system
—you know, practice on an unblemished country, since it
would be hard to do the experiment in our own lands?
Worked fine in Austria (until you look at the cost per cap-
ita, which is still being paid a generation later).

Or should we begin with a pitch of the form, "Say, how
about a 75-mpg runabout that *you* can afford, but built in
your own country on license, all-white, with rental-dropoff
privilege"?

Or maybe just do it like VW and Henry did it, like
Toyota and Nissan are doing it, just build and nourish de-
mand-pull. That should move some 25 million more cars
per year by the end of the decade. Being responsible to
stakeholders in the company-shareholder sense, there's no
question which wins.

No, the responsible solutions will be built for America,
Western Europe, and, to some degree, Japan—and they will
be paradigm-shifting examples that come slowly, unless
Iraq continues to gain ground, so to speak.

But, meanwhile, watch the money being made in the
Third World. And watch the ecosystem pressure build.

NAPIER COLLYNS: My total instinct makes me think that
Chuck is right. Do you all remember the first time you
drove a car? Perhaps as in my case a Dodge-'em car at a fair
or a child's pedal car or even Dinky Toy cars. Driving a car
seems really close to a true basic instinct and we all get
enormous sensual pleasure from driving, and some kind of
deep intellectual satisfaction as well. In Nigeria, people
loved driving cars (though virtually no one had one of their
own) just as much as people do in Los Angeles, where
everyone has one (or two).

7

Trust, Quality, and Labor

●

KEES VAN DER HEIJDEN: Quality has become more and more important as a competitive weapon. A lot depends, of course, on the business you are in and the customer segment you serve, but on average, I think it is fair to say, quality is getting much more attention than even five years ago. Most successful companies that aim to survive in the long run are quality companies. Quality is first of all about building trust between you and your customer. He must feel you will not let him down. Delivering a quality product is obviously a rather essential part of this. But there is more to it.

Someone in this conference made the link between responsibility and trust. A company that does not act responsibly cannot be trusted. So I see a strong link between being a quality company and acting (and being seen to act) "responsibly," whatever that means in the current societal context. That is why I believe that responsibility is good business.

CATHERINE BATESON: Kees, in the U.S., at least, employer-employee relations are not based on trust. Why should I trust a car built in the middle of a battlefield? In that sense, charity/trust begins at home and Japanese corporations have a major advantage.

KEES VAN DER HEIJDEN: Is the average American worker out on the battlefield every day of his life? Can he sustain this? Or has he switched off and is just surviving? Do his company and his job make no contribution to "meaning" in his life?

If this is the reality (I don't know, I have no personal experience in this world), could this be an area which the responsible company would like to reflect upon? Can one company break through this cultural pattern? Is it a realistic objective for a company like Nissan to want to be more to its workers than a weekly wage in this societal desert?

PAMELA McCORDUCK: An interesting question, Kees. But American workers have a built-in distrust of management. The whole scene is conceived of as two adversaries rather than as two sets of teams who both stand to gain.

When I lived in Pittsburgh in the 1970s, people spoke of the Pinkerton agents (called in by Frick to break a strike at the turn of the century) as if the event had happened in everybody's memory. My scanty knowledge of European labor relations says that things were once just as adversarial there, but somehow the Europeans worked it out. Can you offer advice to us?

PETER SCHWARTZ: This is in part the strong antiauthoritarian culture clashing with the imperial nature of management.

DOUG CARMICHAEL: The worker/manager thing is very differentiated. Many workers have more loyalty to the company than managers, and the workers think the managerial strategy for dealing with the future is inadequate to the task. Workers in auto factories are in a sense slave workers. It's still lousy, body-damaging, soul-squeezing work, and it's the punishment for having failed at American society (schooling). On the other hand, many workers love cars and would be partners in any real examination. But it's damn hard to mobilize that concern; the logistics of keeping the line going are overwhelming. Volvo has made some major steps in worker involvement, and there are some hidden aspects to the culture, like ex-auto workers becoming car mechanics. Frequent in Sweden, much less here, because where the factories are is not where the car owners are.

Which leads to another line of thought—many suggestions on what to do, like the modular car approach—may create dangerous and difficult jobs.

JACK HUBER: Kees—interesting point on quality. As Catherine points out, it has been a battlefield out there. For whatever reason, Peter. But there are two changes on the way. Quality is a *big* thing in the U.S. now. We talk about it a lot. If we are going to do anything about it, the adversarial theme must be reduced substantially, if not eliminated. Some have done well—Motorola, Florida Power and Light, Milliken. But many more must make the change or it will be just another trendy thing.

Second point. Knowledge-workers (probably many of us) want to do their work wherever. The work is the thing, and it isn't really work. The company doesn't matter as it once did. "If company A doesn't have what I want, company B or C will, or I'll do it on my own." This has already put a different slant on responsibility and workers in some industries. The quality thing has got to be part of the long-term responsibility. And that does mean trust.

CHUCK HOUSE: This is Chuck House (twenty-nine years at Hewlett-Packard), at least noting that our company has lots of enthusiasm for what the company stands for, and for many of us, being coupled as both management and "labor," and it is not very adversarial as I've known it over the years. So, one American saying not all American companies are like the characterization.

8

Stakeholders Past and Present

●

ART KLEINER: Several other topics have talked about "stakeholders"—the people, besides stockholders, to whom a corporation is responsible. I've been trying to investigate the history of the term. I think I have it traced back to Chester Boulware of General Electric in the late 1940s and early 1950s. Boulware believed in cooperation between the corporation and its employees, including its union employees. Employees were the "stakeholders," along with people who lived near a company, and customers. Unions reviled Boulware and still do; his sense of community was considered a deliberate tactic to undermine collective bargaining and deunionize GE.

CATHERINE BATESON: Art's comment does bring us to questions of differences between U.S. and Japanese management styles.

PAMELA McCORDUCK: I'd like to speak up for those stakeholders who are nearly forgotten in this discussion—those below driving age, and those who, for whatever reasons, cannot drive. I mused earlier (somewhere in this conference) that the basic assumption of nearly all American transportation systems is that, if you cannot drive, you have no business going anywhere. I object to this assumption. And that ties into somebody's astute observation that the idea is to get from place to place, not necessarily to drive. Should the "responsible" company concern itself with this? Maybe not; but we certainly should.

DOUG CARMICHAEL: The increasing number of older people will add to this problem. If, say, 30% of the population is below or above driving-age . . .

STEWART BRAND: Older people with slower reflexes and reduced senses of sight, sound, and motion, plus greater body fragility, are a major, growing "market" and consideration on the streets and highways. Many such, as Pamela mentioned, get big Detroit iron so that, when they do get into an accident, they won't be hurt too badly. This is sensible and realistic of them. (My mother's life was probably saved by the tank-mass she was driving when she rolled through a stoplight and a truck slammed into her.) I'll be sixty-one in the year 2000. I'd like a car that matches whatever faculties I have left then, please.

DOUG CARMICHAEL: While Chuck House's grandchildren are going to school in their '65 VW.